Christian Marriage Conflict Resolution Guide

Biblical Strategies for Effective Communication, Forgiveness, and Strengthening Your Relationship

By

Tiffany Barker

Copyright © 2024 by Tiffany Barker

Publisher: Notemedia Press
First Edition: November, 2024
Scripture quotations are taken from the Holy Bible, New International Version®, NIV®. Copyright © 1973, 1978, 1984, 2011 by Biblica, Inc.™ Used by permission of Zondervan. All rights reserved worldwide. www.zondervan.com The "NIV" and "New International Version" are trademarks registered in the United States Patent and Trademark Office by Biblica, Inc.™

Disclaimer: This book is for informational and educational purposes only. The author and publisher assume no responsibility for any actions taken by readers based on the content provided.

iii

Dedication

To all the couples striving to build a Christ-centered marriage, and to those who have shown me the power of love, patience, and faith. May this guide bring you closer to each other and to God, guiding you through every challenge with hope and grace.

To my spouse who has been my greatest support and source of inspiration on this journey—this book is a testament to our shared faith and love.

With gratitude and love, this is for you.

Acknowledgements

I would like to express my deepest gratitude to all those who supported me in bringing this book to life.

To my family and friends, your unwavering encouragement and love have been a pillar of strength throughout this journey. Your prayers and kind words fueled my commitment to this project, and for that, I am forever grateful.

A special thank you to my spouse whose belief in this book and in me never wavered. Your patience, understanding, and insight have been invaluable in shaping this work.

To my church community and fellow believers, your shared stories, experiences, and wisdom inspired many of the themes explored in these pages. Your dedication to living out your faith in your marriages has shown me what it means to resolve conflicts with grace and humility.

To my pastors, your wisdom and teachings laid the groundwork for this book. Thank you for your guidance and for setting an example of what a strong, faith-driven marriage looks like.

Lastly, to all the couples who have shared their stories and journeys with me—your courage, vulnerability, and faith are what truly make this book possible. May it serve as a testament to the power of love and God's enduring presence in our relationships.

Thank you all for being part of this journey.

Table Of Contents

Foreword

It is an honor to introduce *Christian Marriage Conflict Resolution Guide: Biblical Strategies for Effective Communication, Forgiveness, and Strengthening Your Relationship* by Tiffany Barker. As a pastor and marriage counselor, I have witnessed firsthand how challenges and conflicts can test the bonds of marriage. Yet, I have also seen the transformative power of faith, love, and commitment that allows couples to overcome these trials and grow stronger together.

In today's world, relationships face immense pressures, both from within and outside the home. Couples often struggle to navigate conflicts in a way that honors God and nurtures their connection. This book provides a clear, practical, and faith-based roadmap for resolving conflicts and fostering healthy communication. It reminds us that conflict, when approached with humility and guided by biblical principles, can become an opportunity for growth, healing, and deeper intimacy.

Tiffany Barker has done an exceptional job in intertwining practical advice with scriptural wisdom. Each chapter serves as a tool for couples who are seeking not just resolution but lasting peace and understanding. The inclusion of prayers, reflection questions, and real-life stories brings an added layer of relatability and guidance that many Christian couples will find invaluable.

Whether you are newly married or have been together for decades, this book will remind you of the core truth that a marriage grounded in Christ is resilient. It will encourage you to invite God into your conversations, your challenges, and your moments of forgiveness, allowing His presence to guide and strengthen your bond.

I highly recommend *Christian Marriage Conflict Resolution Guide* as a resource that will bless and uplift any couple committed to building a marriage that reflects God's love and grace.

May you be inspired, encouraged, and transformed as you apply the teachings of this book to your marriage journey.

In His grace,
Pastor David

Preface

Marriage is a sacred bond, designed by God as a union built on love, trust, and faith. Yet, like any profound and meaningful relationship, it comes with its challenges. Throughout my years of working with couples as a Christian author and counselor, I have witnessed the highs of newlywed joy and the lows that accompany unresolved conflict. It is these experiences—both my own and those of countless couples—that have inspired me to write *Christian Marriage Conflict Resolution Guide: Biblical Strategies for Effective Communication, Forgiveness, and Strengthening Your Relationship*.

The motivation for this book stems from my deep belief that conflict, when approached with love, faith, and understanding, does not have to weaken a marriage. Instead, it can be an opportunity for growth, unity, and deeper connection. In my own marriage, I have seen how leaning on God's word and integrating His teachings into our communication can transform disagreements into moments of healing. This personal insight, coupled with years of guiding others through their challenges, has shown me that no marriage is beyond repair when both partners are committed to following Christ's example.

I have written this book with the hope that it serves as both a practical guide and a source of encouragement. Each chapter is rooted in biblical principles and offers realistic, step-by-step advice, prayers, and reflective questions to help couples navigate their challenges. I wanted to create a resource that feels like a conversation with a trusted friend—someone who understands the struggle but also believes wholeheartedly in the strength of a Christ-centered marriage.

This book is dedicated to couples who want more than just survival in their marriage; they want thriving, fulfilling partnerships anchored in faith. Whether you are newly married or have spent decades together, my hope is that the words in these pages will inspire you to approach your conflicts with grace, communicate with love, and forgive with an open heart, all while placing God at the center of your relationship.

I invite you to take this journey with me—to reflect, learn, and grow in your faith and your marriage. With God's help, you can build a partnership that not only withstands the storms but becomes stronger because of them.

With faith and love,
Tiffany Barker

Christian Marriage Conflict Resolution Guide

Biblical Strategies for Effective Communication, Forgiveness, and Strengthening Your Relationship

Introduction

Marriage is one of God's most beautiful gifts, uniting two people in love, commitment, and shared faith. Yet, like any relationship, marriage comes with its own set of challenges, and conflict is a natural part of that journey. Christian Marriage Conflict Resolution Guide: Biblical Strategies for Effective Communication, Forgiveness, and Strengthening Your Relationship was created to help you approach these challenges with grace, transforming difficult moments into opportunities to strengthen your bond and grow in understanding.

This guide is for couples who want to deepen their relationship while staying firmly rooted in Christian faith. While many resources on marriage offer useful advice, few provide guidance grounded in biblical teachings. This book combines practical, everyday strategies with God's wisdom to help you resolve conflicts, improve communication, and build a stronger, more loving partnership. My hope is that this book will be a supportive companion, offering guidance as you grow together in love and faith.

Purpose of the Book

The main purpose of this guide is to show you that conflict doesn't have to drive you apart; instead, it can bring you closer together. Through the lens of Christian values, this book will help you turn disagreements into opportunities for learning and connection. With tools and insights that align with your faith, you'll find ways to transform conflict into moments of growth and deepen your mutual understanding and respect.

This book is designed to walk you through practical ways of handling conflict and communicating more effectively, all while keeping God at the center of your relationship. Whether you're facing significant challenges or simply looking to improve daily conversations, these teachings are here to support you on your journey.

How to Use This Guide

This guide is meant to be simple, practical, and easy to apply in real life. Here's how to make the most of it:

- **Read with an Open Heart**

Approach each chapter with a readiness to learn and grow. Whether you're newly married or have been together for many years, these pages are here to meet you wherever you are on your journey.

- **Engage in the Activities**

Throughout the book, you'll find exercises, thought-provoking questions, and actionable steps. These activities are designed to help you put what you've learned into practice in your marriage. Take your time with each exercise—there's no rush, only a steady path toward growth.

- **Pray and Reflect**

You'll encounter prayers and Bible verses throughout the book, offering ways to invite God into your journey. Use these moments to pray individually or together, helping you keep your focus on Him and allowing His guidance to shape your relationship.

- **Share with Your Spouse**

Discussing the insights and tips from this book can be a meaningful way to connect. Set aside time to talk about what you're learning and how you can apply it in daily life. These conversations can deepen your bond and build shared understanding.

- **Return as Needed**

Conflicts and challenges in marriage evolve over time. This book is here for you whenever you need a reminder, encouragement, or guidance. Revisit chapters as new situations arise, using the principles to support you both.

With these practical tips, prayers, and teachings, you can approach conflicts in a way that brings you and your spouse closer together, while also strengthening your faith. Let this book serve as a reminder that, with God's help, every challenge is an opportunity to grow as a couple. Together, you can build a marriage that reflects God's love, patience, and peace, navigating both the joys and trials hand in hand.

Chapter 1

Embracing Conflict in Christian Marriage

Conflict is an unavoidable part of any close relationship, including marriage. For many, it's a word that brings unease, often associated with friction and discomfort. However, when viewed from a broader perspective, conflict is more than just a hurdle; it's a complex, layered experience that reveals each partner's individuality and the unique blend of perspectives, histories, and expectations they bring into the marriage.

At its root, conflict is what happens when desires, needs, or viewpoints don't align. This can be as simple as differing opinions on handling finances or as complex as deeply held beliefs about parenting or family roles. Each partner enters marriage with a lifetime of personal experiences, values, and habits that shape who they are and how they approach life. Even in a marriage where both partners share a commitment to their Christian faith, these differences are bound to surface.

Take, for instance, the way a husband and wife might approach a financial decision. One partner may be deeply practical, influenced by a family background that values saving and careful budgeting, while the other might be more spontaneous, seeing financial resources as an opportunity for enjoyment and enrichment. Both views have merit, yet without an understanding of each other's perspectives, these differences can quickly create tension.

Another source of conflict can be found in communication styles. One partner might be more direct, preferring to address issues head-on, while the other might lean toward subtle hints, hoping that emotions and cues will be enough to convey a message. Without recognizing these differences, misunderstandings can easily arise, creating a sense of disconnection or frustration. It's in these subtle day-to-day interactions that many conflicts begin, often unnoticed until they grow into something larger.

Sometimes, conflict stems not from what is said but from what is left unspoken. Silence, especially when it hides underlying frustrations or disappointments, can create a distance that builds over time. When communication is avoided, feelings of hurt or resentment may simmer just below the surface, waiting for a moment to emerge, often in the form of unexpected outbursts. **In James 1:19, we are reminded to be "quick to listen, slow to speak, and slow to become angry" (NIV).** This wisdom emphasizes the idea that conflicts often start in moments when we react before fully understanding one another. Listening deeply and without assumption can transform moments of tension into opportunities for connection.

External pressures, such as financial strain, work stress, or family obligations, can also amplify conflict within a marriage. These stresses can make small disagreements feel like much larger issues, as each partner's ability to handle tension may be worn down by the weight of outside burdens. In these times, it's crucial to recognize that the conflict isn't necessarily about the immediate issue at hand but often about a larger sense of feeling overwhelmed. Learning to identify these stressors and understanding how they influence reactions can help couples see conflict more clearly and respond with compassion.

Furthermore, each partner's natural response to tension can play a role in how conflicts unfold. Some individuals may become defensive, feeling the need to protect their viewpoint, while others might withdraw, hoping that the issue will fade if left unaddressed. These reactions, while understandable, rarely lead to resolution. Instead, they create a cycle where each person feels unheard or invalidated. Recognizing and accepting each other's natural responses can open the door to healthier ways of handling disagreements, helping both partners see conflict not as a threat but as an opportunity to understand each other more deeply.

In a Christian marriage, conflict takes on an additional layer of significance. There is a biblical call to maintain love, respect, and unity, even in moments of disagreement. Conflict, though challenging, is also a time to practice the virtues of patience, kindness, and forgiveness, as described in 1 Corinthians 13:4-7. These verses remind us that love isn't just a feeling; it's a commitment that shapes how we respond to our spouse, especially in moments of difficulty. When viewed through this lens, conflict becomes less about winning or proving a point and more about nurturing a relationship that reflects Christ's love.

Understanding conflict as a natural and potentially constructive part of marriage can change the way we approach it. Rather than seeing it as a failure or a sign of discord, couples can begin to recognize it as a moment of growth—a chance to learn more about each other and themselves. Every disagreement holds the potential to either build walls or create bridges, depending on how it is approached. By seeing conflict as an opportunity to connect and grow, couples can transform arguments into meaningful conversations, building a marriage based on mutual understanding, respect, and faith.

The Role of Conflict in Strengthening a Marriage

Conflict in marriage often brings to mind discomfort, yet it has the potential to be a powerful tool for growth and unity. For many couples, the idea that disagreements can deepen love and strengthen a bond might seem contradictory. However, when viewed through the lens of faith, conflict becomes an opportunity for deeper communication, mutual respect, and spiritual growth. In Christian marriages, understanding that conflict has a purpose beyond temporary frustration is key to approaching challenges with love, patience, and wisdom.

First, conflict can act as a channel for honest communication. During disagreements, couples are often more inclined to express thoughts and feelings that may not surface in everyday conversations. These moments allow both partners to look beyond routine exchanges and truly engage with each other's deeper values and emotions. For example, imagine a scenario where one partner feels overlooked or misunderstood regarding family decisions. A disagreement about this can lead to an honest discussion, where both can share not just their thoughts but their underlying hopes or fears. These transparent conversations build trust and affirm a commitment to addressing issues rather than avoiding them. **Proverbs 27:17 reminds us, "As iron sharpens iron, so one person sharpens another" (NIV).** This verse beautifully illustrates how even the friction in relationships can refine and strengthen both individuals, encouraging them to grow together with love and respect.

Conflict also acts as a mirror, revealing areas for personal growth and change. Every disagreement brings to light habits or behaviors that may be unhelpful or even hurtful. For example, if one partner often responds to tension defensively, conflict may highlight this tendency, providing an opportunity for self-reflection and growth. By addressing these behaviors, couples can develop emotional maturity, which fosters a more balanced and harmonious relationship. When both partners approach conflict with patience, they build resilience and strengthen their commitment to one another. In this way, conflict becomes less about division and more about learning how to understand and respect each other's individuality.

Another significant role of conflict in a Christian marriage is as a path to spiritual growth. Disagreements can be times when couples are drawn to prayer and God's guidance, relying on Him to help them find peace and understanding. Seeking God's wisdom during these moments not only brings resolution but also strengthens faith, reminding both partners that their marriage is a covenant that includes God at its center. When couples come together in prayer, asking for patience and understanding, they invite God's presence into their relationship in a powerful way. This spiritual connection not only helps to resolve the immediate issue but builds a deeper reliance on God that reinforces the marriage as a whole.

Conflict also strengthens marriage by teaching the values of compromise and empathy. It's easy to cling to one's own viewpoint during disagreements, expecting the other person to concede. Yet true resolution requires both partners to actively seek each other's perspective and to find common ground. This act of seeking a middle path isn't just a practical solution—it's an expression of love and respect. Philippians 2:3 advises, "Do nothing out of selfish ambition or vain conceit. Rather, in humility value others above yourselves" (NIV). Applying this teaching in marriage helps both partners move beyond "winning" an argument to prioritizing the relationship, fostering a deeper bond that values unity over individual pride.

Forgiveness and grace are additional gifts that conflict offers to a marriage. Every marriage will experience moments when words are spoken in frustration or decisions are made that hurt the other person. These instances offer an opportunity to practice forgiveness, an essential component of any strong relationship. Forgiveness isn't just for the person who receives it; it's a choice that frees both partners from resentment, allowing them to let go of the past and rebuild their connection. **Ephesians 4:32 reminds us to "be kind and compassionate to one another, forgiving each other, just as in Christ God forgave you" (NIV).** This verse beautifully encapsulates the call to approach our spouse with the same grace that God extends to us, even in our imperfections. Through forgiveness, couples can turn painful moments into stepping stones toward greater unity.

Commitment is another crucial element that is strengthened through conflict. Every marriage will face times when disagreements feel overwhelming. Yet choosing to stay engaged and work through these challenges together reaffirms the promise made to stand by each other, through every season of life. These moments can be deeply transformative, showing both partners that their love is resilient, capable of withstanding adversity. The very act of facing and overcoming conflict together builds trust, proving that they are committed to each other in every sense.

Finally, conflicts provide a foundation for continuous learning. Each disagreement offers insights into how to communicate better, understand each other more deeply, and grow spiritually. This ongoing process equips couples to handle future challenges with greater wisdom and patience, making their marriage stronger and more resilient over time. It's an evolving journey of growth, where each lesson learned enriches the relationship. Embracing this perspective allows couples to see conflict not as a series of problems to be solved but as part of the process of building a strong, faith-filled marriage.

Key Bible Verses About Conflict

Navigating conflict in a marriage can be challenging, but the Bible offers guidance that grounds our responses in patience, love, and understanding. Each of these verses provides a timeless reminder that with God's wisdom, we can transform conflict into moments of growth, connection, and healing. Let's explore how these scriptures speak to the heart of managing disagreements in a faith-filled marriage.

"A gentle answer turns away wrath, but a harsh word stirs up anger." (Proverbs 15:1, NIV)

This verse beautifully emphasizes the power of our words during moments of tension. In a conflict, our natural impulse might be to respond sharply, especially when emotions are high. Yet Proverbs reminds us of the calming effect of gentleness. A soft answer has the power to ease tension, inviting both partners into a space of mutual respect and understanding. Imagine a situation where frustration could easily escalate into anger—a gentle response can shift the atmosphere, allowing each person to share their feelings openly without fear of escalation.

"My dear brothers and sisters, take note of this: Everyone should be quick to listen, slow to speak and slow to become angry." (James 1:19, NIV)

In marriage, listening is a profound act of love. James emphasizes the importance of patience and attentiveness, especially in times of disagreement. When we rush to speak or react, we may miss the heart of what our partner is trying to express. This verse calls us to listen fully, giving our spouse the space to be heard and understood. By taking time to listen first, we create an environment where both partners feel respected and valued, reducing the likelihood of misunderstandings that can fuel conflict.

"In your anger do not sin: Do not let the sun go down while you are still angry." (Ephesians 4:26, NIV)

This verse acknowledges that anger is a natural human response but cautions us to manage it wisely. Allowing anger to linger can lead to resentment, which can create lasting distance between partners. Ephesians advises us to address disagreements before the end of the day, encouraging reconciliation and maintaining both emotional and spiritual closeness. Imagine ending each day with unresolved tension versus choosing to seek peace—it makes a lasting difference in the overall health of the relationship.

"Bear with each other and forgive one another if any of you has a grievance against someone. Forgive as the Lord forgave you." (Colossians 3:13, NIV)

Forgiveness is foundational to a strong and lasting marriage. This verse reminds us to approach our spouse with grace, mirroring the forgiveness that God freely gives to us. Holding onto grievances can erode trust and intimacy over time, while forgiveness opens the door for healing and unity. Forgiveness doesn't mean we ignore or forget the hurt; rather, it's a conscious choice to release resentment and move forward together. This commitment to grace allows couples to rebuild connection even after moments of hurt.

"Do nothing out of selfish ambition or vain conceit. Rather, in humility value others above yourselves." (Philippians 2:3, NIV)

Conflict can bring out the instinct to protect our pride or defend our position. However, this verse encourages humility, asking us to prioritize our spouse's needs and perspectives over our own desire to "win" an argument. When we approach conflict with a humble heart, willing to see from the other's viewpoint, we transform disagreements into moments of mutual respect and growth. **Philippians 2:3** challenges us to embrace a selfless attitude, reminding us that the bond between partners is more important than being right.

"Blessed are the peacemakers, for they will be called children of God." (Matthew 5:9, NIV)

In every conflict, there is an opportunity to choose peace. This verse calls us to actively pursue reconciliation, even when it feels difficult. Peacemaking in marriage is a daily choice that reflects God's love and grace. Rather than waiting for peace to happen, we're encouraged to take intentional steps toward harmony. By becoming peacemakers, we not only foster unity within our marriage but also honor our calling as followers of Christ, letting His love be the foundation of our relationship.

"Starting a quarrel is like breaching a dam; so drop the matter before a dispute breaks out." (Proverbs 17:14, NIV)

Discernment is essential in marriage, especially when determining which issues are worth pursuing and which are best left alone. This verse emphasizes the wisdom of knowing when to let go. Some conflicts can be avoided altogether by recognizing that certain disagreements may not be as significant as they seem in the moment. Proverbs encourages us to prevent unnecessary disputes, keeping minor issues from escalating and maintaining peace within the relationship.

"Husbands, in the same way be considerate as you live with your wives, and treat them with respect as the weaker partner and as heirs with you of the gracious gift of life, so that nothing will hinder your prayers." (1 Peter 3:7, NIV)

Although directed at husbands, this verse speaks to the importance of mutual respect in marriage. Consideration, understanding, and respect are essential for both partners, especially during disagreements. By treating each other with respect, even in times of tension, couples ensure that their relationship remains spiritually sound and grounded in love. Respectful treatment fosters trust, allowing both partners to feel safe and valued, which ultimately strengthens the bond they share.

Chapter 2
Communication Essentials for a Stronger Bond

In a marriage, communication isn't simply about exchanging words; it's the lifeline that nurtures intimacy and understanding. When communication is strong, it serves as a bridge that connects two hearts, allowing each person to feel seen, heard, and valued. However, for many couples, communication can become transactional or reactive, rather than intentional and heartfelt. One of the most profound ways to safeguard this connection is through active listening—a practice that goes beyond hearing words to truly understanding the heart behind them.

Active listening is a commitment to be fully present with your spouse, showing that their words and emotions are important to you. It means setting aside distractions, engaging with what they're saying, and responding in a way that shows you understand. When your spouse feels that they are genuinely heard, it reinforces trust and creates a safe space for open, meaningful dialogue. In a Christian marriage, this kind of listening reflects Christ's patience and compassion, who always made space for those who sought Him, no matter how busy or burdened He was.

The Art of Being Fully Present

Active listening begins with a choice to set aside distractions—whether it's the television, a phone, or other tasks. When we shift our attention completely to our spouse, we're communicating that they have our full focus and that their words are valued. Eye contact, for example, is a simple yet powerful way to signal attentiveness. Just as Jesus looked at those He spoke with, showing them that He cared about their struggles and joys, making eye contact with your spouse can deepen your connection and foster mutual respect.

Engaged listening also involves small but meaningful responses like nodding, or giving verbal cues such as, **"I understand"** or **"I see."** These signals let your spouse know you're following along, making them feel respected and appreciated. In a culture that often encourages multitasking, these small gestures become acts of love, offering our undivided attention in a way that strengthens our bond.

Reflecting and Summarizing with Empathy

Another vital part of active listening is reflecting back what you've heard. This doesn't mean simply repeating words, but rather summarizing your spouse's thoughts in your own words to show that you truly understand. For example, if your spouse says, **"I feel overwhelmed when I don't get help with the household chores,"** you might respond with, **"It sounds like you're feeling stressed when the responsibilities pile up. Is that right?"** This kind of response shows empathy and lets your spouse know that you're not only hearing their words but also grasping the emotions behind them.

This practice also provides an opportunity for clarification. If there's any ambiguity, gently ask for more details. Phrases like, **"Can you help me understand that better?" or "What do you mean when you say…?"** invite your spouse to share more openly. This deepens the conversation and encourages a sense of safety where they feel comfortable expressing themselves fully. In Proverbs 18:13, we're reminded, **"To answer before listening—that is folly and shame" (NIV).** Taking time to fully understand before responding allows us to honor our spouse with attentiveness and humility.

Speaking with Intention and Purpose

While listening forms one side of the communication coin, speaking with intention completes it. Speaking with intention means choosing words thoughtfully, aiming to build a bridge rather than a wall. When addressing a concern or sharing your feelings, use words that foster connection rather than division. For instance, statements like **"You never help around the house"** can feel like accusations, putting your spouse on the defensive. Instead, consider using **"I"** statements, such as, **"I feel overwhelmed when I manage the chores alone."** This subtle shift allows you to express your feelings without attributing blame, inviting your spouse to understand rather than defend.

Tone of voice is equally important. Words that are delivered gently and kindly are far more likely to be received well than words that are harsh or abrupt. **Proverbs 15:1 teaches us, "A gentle answer turns away wrath, but a harsh word stirs up anger" (NIV).** Even when we have something important or difficult to say, our tone can make a tremendous difference. By speaking calmly and kindly, we foster a climate of understanding, making it easier for our spouse to hear the heart behind our words.

Choosing the Right Moment

Timing can make all the difference in how our words are received. Attempting to discuss serious issues when one partner is tired, stressed, or distracted can lead to misunderstandings or missed messages. Waiting for a moment when both partners can give their full attention to the conversation can make discussions more productive and compassionate. Jesus demonstrated this wisdom by knowing when to speak and when to remain silent, showing us that discernment in timing is part of effective communication.

Choosing the right time also reflects a respect for our spouse's mental and emotional space. Rather than addressing issues at a time when emotions are high, waiting for a calm moment can pave the way for a thoughtful, respectful conversation. **As Ecclesiastes 3:7 reminds us, there is "a time to be silent and a time to speak" (NIV).**

Patience and Respect in Communication

Effective communication also requires patience. Each of us has a unique way of expressing our thoughts and feelings. Some might need more time to articulate what's on their mind, while others may process emotions differently. By showing patience, we create a space where our spouse feels valued, knowing they won't be rushed or dismissed. This patience, especially when our spouse struggles to find the right words, is a powerful expression of love and respect.

In marriage, our goal isn't to **"win"** a conversation or prove our point. Instead, it's to create an environment where both partners feel valued and understood. By combining active listening and intentional speaking, we foster a relationship where conflicts become less about taking sides and more about seeking unity and growth. This shift in perspective turns conversations from potential battlegrounds into opportunities to strengthen the bond between spouses.

Pitfalls to Avoid and Maintaining Respectful Communication

Even with the best intentions, communication in marriage can sometimes drift off course. Recognizing common pitfalls and understanding how to avoid them can make a meaningful difference in keeping dialogue respectful, compassionate, and constructive. Here, we explore some of the most frequent challenges couples face in communication and practical ways to steer clear of these stumbling blocks.

a. Interrupting the Flow

One major pitfall in communication is the tendency to interrupt, especially during intense or emotional moments. It's a habit that often arises when we feel compelled to defend our viewpoint or clarify our intentions. Yet, interruption can signal to our spouse that their thoughts and feelings are not as valuable as our own, making them feel dismissed or unheard. **James 1:19 reminds us to be "quick to listen, slow to speak and slow to become angry" (NIV).** In practice, this wisdom encourages us to pause, take a breath, and allow our partner to complete their thoughts before responding.

If you feel the urge to jump in, try silently repeating a phrase like **"listen first."** This simple pause allows the conversation to flow naturally, showing your spouse that their words are valued. Remember, listening fully before speaking fosters mutual respect and sets the stage for genuine understanding.

b. Avoiding Assumptions

Another common pitfall in communication is making assumptions about what our partner means. Without realizing it, we may project our own feelings or insecurities onto their words, leading to unnecessary misunderstandings. For example, if your spouse says, **"I'm tired of handling everything by myself,"** it's easy to assume they are criticizing your contribution. However, they may simply be expressing their own exhaustion. Rather than assuming, try responding with empathy and curiosity, such as, **"I hear that you're feeling tired. Would you like to talk about how we can share things more evenly?"**

This approach not only clears up assumptions but also invites a supportive conversation, helping both partners feel validated and understood. **Proverbs 18:13 tells us, "To answer before listening—that is folly and shame" (NIV).** By seeking clarification, we show a willingness to understand our spouse's true intentions, fostering a sense of safety in the dialogue.

c. Raising Your Voice or Using a Harsh Tone

The tone we use in conversation speaks volumes. While it's natural to feel frustrated during difficult discussions, allowing that frustration to seep into our tone can quickly shut down communication. Yelling, sharp words, or a harsh tone can make our spouse feel attacked, leading them to either become defensive or withdraw entirely.

To avoid this, practice calming techniques before responding. Taking a deep breath, lowering your voice, or briefly pausing can transform the atmosphere of a conversation. **Proverbs 15:1 reminds us, "A gentle answer turns away wrath, but a harsh word stirs up anger" (NIV).** When we approach our spouse with gentleness, even in challenging conversations, we create a space where they feel safe to share openly. This gentleness allows for a productive exchange, where both partners feel heard and respected.

d. Avoiding Blame and Embracing "I" Statements

Blame is another common barrier to healthy communication. Beginning a sentence with **"You always"** or **"You never"** often feels like an accusation, causing our spouse to become defensive. These statements can spiral a conversation into arguments rather than fostering understanding. Instead, using "I" statements allows us to express our feelings without placing blame.

For example, saying, **"I feel overwhelmed when I manage the chores alone"** rather than **"You never help around the house"** shifts the focus to how we feel and what we need. This change in language invites compassion and cooperation rather than defensiveness, promoting a sense of teamwork. **In Ephesians 4:29, we are encouraged to "speak only what is helpful for building others up according to their needs" (NIV).** By framing our words thoughtfully, we open the door to a more loving and constructive conversation.

e. Mindfulness of Nonverbal Communication

Nonverbal communication often speaks louder than words. Body language, facial expressions, and eye contact all convey messages, whether intended or not. Actions like crossing arms, rolling eyes, or turning away from our partner can signal frustration or disinterest, even if our words are neutral. In marriage, paying attention to these cues can significantly impact how our spouse perceives our intentions.

Try to maintain open body language by facing your partner, maintaining gentle eye contact, and nodding when appropriate. This openness shows that you are engaged and willing to work through the issue together. Just as we should be mindful of our words, being conscious of our body language ensures that our spouse feels respected and valued in every interaction.

f. Defensiveness as a Roadblock to Understanding

Defensiveness is a natural reaction, especially when we feel accused or misunderstood. However, it diverts the conversation from the issue at hand to a stance of self-protection, making it difficult to find meaningful solutions. If your spouse says, **"I feel like we haven't been spending enough time together,"** a defensive response might be, **"Well, I'm busy working hard for this family!"** This reply deflects from their concern, turning the focus toward defending yourself rather than addressing the issue.

A better approach is to acknowledge your spouse's feelings and express a willingness to understand. Responding with something like**, "I didn't realize you felt that way. How can we make more time for each other?"** shows empathy and opens the door to finding solutions together. When we choose understanding over defensiveness, we strengthen the bond and demonstrate respect for our partner's perspective.

g. Avoiding Stonewalling and Remaining Present

Stonewalling, or withdrawing from a conversation, is a common reaction when we feel overwhelmed or frustrated. While taking a moment to gather our thoughts can be beneficial, completely shutting down communication leaves issues unresolved and can make our spouse feel abandoned. If you need time to cool down, communicate that clearly: **"I need a moment to think, but I want to come back and talk this through."**

This approach shows your spouse that while you may need space, you are committed to resolving the issue together. By balancing personal reflection with a willingness to re-engage, you reinforce the trust that underpins your relationship.

Maintaining respectful communication in marriage means consistently choosing compassion over quick reactions, understanding over assumption, and love over pride. A respectful approach not only values our spouse's perspective, even if it differs from our own, but it also builds a foundation of trust and love that sustains future conversations. By avoiding these common pitfalls, you can cultivate a style of communication that strengthens your relationship and deepens your connection.

As you practice thoughtful, respectful communication, you'll find that each conversation handled with care contributes to a more harmonious, resilient bond. These small, intentional adjustments—pausing before responding, asking for clarification, being mindful of nonverbal cues—add up to a relationship that's marked by mutual respect, empathy, and love.

Bible-Based Guidance on Communication (Ephesians 4:29)

In a Christian marriage, effective communication is more than just choosing the right words—it's about reflecting faith, love, and mutual respect in every conversation. Scripture provides timeless wisdom on how to approach communication in a way that builds each other up, fostering a relationship grounded in grace and unity. **Ephesians 4:29 (NIV) offers a powerful foundation: "Do not let any unwholesome talk come out of your mouths, but only what is helpful for building others up according to their needs, that it may benefit those who listen."** This verse serves as a guide, calling us to choose words that uplift and strengthen our marriage, rather than words that might harm or create distance.

a. Guarding Against Unwholesome Talk

The first part of Ephesians 4:29, **"Do not let any unwholesome talk come out of your mouths,"** reminds couples of the need to be mindful of their words. Harsh comments, sarcasm, or criticism—even when unintended—can create lasting rifts in a marriage. Words spoken in frustration can often be hurtful, yet the Bible encourages us to express our feelings in ways that build rather than tear down. When emotions run high, it's natural to feel the urge to speak impulsively, but taking a moment to pause and consider whether our words will heal or hurt can make all the difference.

Consider framing your words with respect, even during disagreement. Instead of saying, **"You never help with anything around here,"** try **"I feel overwhelmed when I handle everything on my own."** This subtle shift helps convey your feelings without placing blame, inviting your spouse to listen rather than react defensively. **Proverbs 15:4 (NIV) reminds us, "The soothing tongue is a tree of life, but a perverse tongue crushes the spirit."** This verse emphasizes the power of words to either bring life and encouragement or to wound and divide. In marriage, choosing words that heal and nurture strengthens the bond and invites God's peace into the relationship.

b. Building Each Other Up According to Their Needs

The next part of **Ephesians 4:29, "but only what is helpful for building others up according to their needs,"** highlights the importance of speaking in ways that meet our spouse's emotional and spiritual needs. This approach requires a shift from simply expressing our own feelings to considering what our spouse may need in that moment. Are they seeking comfort, validation, or encouragement? By tailoring our words to offer what they need, we reinforce the foundation of love and support within the marriage.

For example, if your spouse shares feelings of discouragement, responding with **"I'm here for you, and I believe in you"** can be more uplifting than offering unsolicited advice or dismissing their feelings. Acknowledging their perspective with affirming statements like, **"I**

appreciate that you shared this with me" or "I can see why this is **important to you"** makes your spouse feel valued and respected. As **Proverbs 16:24 (NIV) says, "Gracious words are a honeycomb, sweet to the soul and healing to the bones."** By speaking with kindness and empathy, we create an environment where both partners feel supported and encouraged.

c. Ensuring Words Benefit Those Who Listen

The final part of Ephesians 4:29, **"that it may benefit those who listen,"** reminds us to make our conversations constructive and uplifting. Rather than speaking out of anger, frustration, or the desire to win, this verse encourages us to communicate with the intention of benefiting both partners, fostering mutual understanding, and nurturing peace. In a marriage, the goal of communication is not merely to express one's own thoughts but to ensure that each exchange strengthens the relationship.

When facing challenging topics, approach the conversation with a mindset of resolution and unity. Avoid conversations driven by frustration or irritation, and instead focus on finding solutions together. Speaking with the intention of building each other up reflects the love that defines a Christ-centered marriage, aligning with the principle of love and unity found in scripture. **As Colossians 4:6 (NIV) advises, "Let your conversation be always full of grace, seasoned with salt, so that you may know how to answer everyone."** This grace-filled approach transforms communication into a source of connection and understanding, even during difficult discussions.

Complementary Verses on Communication

Several other verses offer additional guidance on how to communicate with love and respect:

Proverbs 15:1 (NIV): "A gentle answer turns away wrath, but a harsh word stirs up anger." This verse reinforces the importance of tone in communication. A gentle response can de-escalate potential conflict, creating a safe environment for both partners to share openly. Practicing gentleness, even in disagreement, fosters trust and makes it easier for your spouse to receive your words.

James 1:19 (NIV): "Everyone should be quick to listen, slow to speak and slow to become angry." James calls us to listen attentively before responding, valuing our partner's perspective. By being "quick to listen," we show our spouse that we respect their viewpoint and are open to understanding. This approach sets the stage for a calm, loving exchange that brings clarity and prevents misunderstanding.

1 Corinthians 13:4-7 (NIV): "Love is patient, love is kind… it is not easily angered, it keeps no record of wrongs." This passage beautifully describes love as patient, kind, and forgiving—qualities that should infuse every conversation in marriage. Practicing patience, kindness, and forgiveness in our communication reflects the love God has for us and helps ensure that our words are wrapped in grace.

These verses together create a blueprint for respectful and constructive communication. When we approach each conversation with a commitment to listen, respond thoughtfully, and speak with kindness, we create a marriage environment that fosters peace and intimacy.

Practical Steps to Apply Bible-Based Communication

Applying these biblical teachings can reshape how you and your spouse communicate, making each interaction a reflection of Christ's love. Here are a few practical steps to incorporate these insights into daily conversations:

- **Pause Before Speaking**: Take a brief moment to consider your words. This pause helps you check whether your response aligns with the principles of kindness, respect, and love.
- **Use "I" Statements**: Frame your thoughts with "I" statements to express your feelings without assigning blame. Statements like, "I feel concerned when…" allow you to share honestly while showing respect for your partner's perspective.
- **Focus on Understanding**: Prioritize listening over speaking. Allow your spouse to share their thoughts fully before responding. When your spouse feels truly heard, it creates a stronger sense of trust and connection.
- **Pray for Guidance**: Ask God to help you communicate with love and patience. Prayer invites the Holy Spirit to work within your heart, guiding your words and calming any frustration or impatience.
- **Practice Gentleness**: Use a gentle tone and nonverbal cues like eye contact to show that you are fully present. Gentleness can soften difficult conversations and make your spouse feel valued and respected.

In a Christian marriage, communication shaped by scripture is a powerful tool for deepening love and understanding. Letting verses like Ephesians 4:29 guide your conversations fosters a relationship where words are used to uplift, heal, and bring joy. By embracing the Bible's teachings on communication, you create a foundation of faith and respect that helps you both grow closer to each other and to God. When conversations are grounded in love and humility, they become opportunities to reflect Christ's love, bringing you and your spouse together in ways that strengthen your bond and bring lasting peace to your marriage.

Key Takeaways: Quick Tips for Effective Communication

Maintaining strong, open, and loving communication is at the heart of a thriving Christian marriage. While exploring biblical principles and communication strategies in depth is valuable, having a set of quick, actionable tips can make it easier to apply these insights in everyday conversations. Here are key takeaways to help you build respectful and effective communication, supporting a marriage that reflects God's love.

- **Listen Before You Speak**

Make it a habit to listen with the intent to understand, not just to respond. Listening deeply to your spouse's words, thoughts, and feelings before sharing your own encourages trust and reduces the likelihood of misunderstandings. When we listen first, we honor their voice, creating a space where they feel truly valued.

- **Use "I" Statements**

xpressing feelings with "I" statements, like "I feel…" or "I need…," allows you to share your emotions without sounding accusatory. For example, saying "I feel hurt when…" rather than "You always…" avoids blame and shifts the focus from fault to understanding. This approach fosters collaboration rather than defensiveness, making it easier to work through challenges together.

- **Watch Your Tone**

The tone in which we speak can completely change the meaning of our words. A calm and gentle voice, even in difficult moments, communicates respect and care. Proverbs 15:1 (NIV) reminds us, "A gentle answer turns away wrath, but a harsh word stirs up anger." By approaching conversations with gentleness, we create an atmosphere where both partners feel safe and respected.

- **Choose Words Wisely**

Before speaking, take a moment to consider whether your words will build up or tear down. Ephesians 4:29 (NIV) guides us, "Do not let any unwholesome talk come out of your mouths, but only what is helpful for building others up according to their needs." Strive to choose words that uplift and encourage your spouse, even during disagreements. Loving words strengthen the bond between you, reminding both partners of the shared commitment to build each other up.

- **Maintain Eye Contact and Open Body Language**

Nonverbal communication is just as important as spoken words. Facing your spouse, maintaining eye contact, and using open body language demonstrate that you are fully present and engaged. These subtle cues convey respect and attentiveness, showing your spouse that they have your complete attention.

- **Avoid Interrupting**

Interruptions can make your spouse feel dismissed or unheard. Letting them finish their thoughts before responding demonstrates patience and respect, reinforcing that their perspective matters to you. When both partners feel safe to share without interruption, it creates an environment where open and honest communication flourishes.

-

- **Stay Focused on the Topic at Hand**

When discussing an issue, avoid the temptation to bring up past grievances or unrelated topics. Bringing up unrelated concerns can derail the conversation and create confusion. Focusing on one issue at a time keeps the dialogue clear and productive, allowing you to reach a meaningful resolution.

- **Take Breaks if Emotions Run High**

When emotions become overwhelming, it's okay to pause the conversation. Taking a short break can help both partners gather their thoughts and return with a clearer mind. Be sure to communicate that you're taking a moment and that you plan to revisit the discussion soon. This approach shows respect for each other's emotional state while reinforcing the commitment to resolve the issue.

- **Express Appreciation**

Even during challenging discussions, take time to express gratitude for your spouse. Acknowledging their efforts or positive traits, even in the midst of a disagreement, reminds both of you that the relationship is rooted in love and respect. Appreciation can soften tense moments and provide a positive perspective that helps navigate through conflict with grace.

▪ Pray Together Before Tough Conversations

Inviting God into your conversations by praying together before tackling serious topics can set a tone of faith and respect. Starting with prayer brings peace and reminds both partners that their relationship is rooted in shared faith. It can transform the atmosphere, turning a difficult discussion into an opportunity for spiritual connection and mutual growth.

▪ Ask Clarifying Questions

If you're unsure of your spouse's meaning, don't hesitate to ask for clarification. Simple questions like, "Can you explain that a bit more?" or "What did you mean when you said…?" show that you care about understanding fully. This curiosity fosters a sense of safety, where your spouse feels free to share honestly.

▪ Be Willing to Apologize

Admitting when you're wrong and offering a sincere apology can defuse tension and build trust. An honest apology shows humility and prioritizes the relationship over personal pride. This simple act of repentance can open the door to healing, reaffirming the love and respect you have for one another.

▪ Reiterate What You've Heard

Paraphrasing or repeating back what your spouse has shared can ensure understanding and help them feel heard. For instance, saying, "So, what I'm hearing is that you feel…" confirms that you are both on the same page and can help avoid misunderstandings. This practice fosters mutual respect and sets the tone for productive, heartfelt dialogue.

- **Set Boundaries for Healthy Conversations**
  Establish guidelines to keep discussions respectful and focused. Simple rules, such as avoiding name-calling, sarcasm, or speaking over each other, create a safe space where both partners feel comfortable sharing openly. Boundaries encourage respect and make it easier to have honest, effective communication.

- **Let Scripture Guide Your Words**
  Use scripture as a compass for your conversations. Verses like James 1:19 (NIV), "Everyone should be quick to listen, slow to speak and slow to become angry," provide a powerful reminder of God's wisdom in our everyday interactions. Letting the Bible shape your communication fosters a relationship built on the principles of love, patience, and kindness.

Applying these key tips will help you maintain a pattern of positive, respectful communication that reflects the teachings of scripture. When conversations are rooted in respect, patience, and love, couples can face challenges together, strengthen their bond, and ensure that their marriage mirrors the love of Christ. By embracing these quick yet meaningful practices, you'll create a foundation of trust and understanding that helps navigate even the most challenging discussions with grace and unity.

Chapter 3

The Power and Practice of Forgiveness

Why Forgiveness Is Essential for Healing and Growth

Forgiveness is one of the most transformative tools in building a lasting marriage. It's more than just saying, "I'm sorry," or choosing to move past a disagreement. True forgiveness means releasing resentment and anger, even when those emotions feel justified. It's a decision to let go of hurt and choose peace and reconciliation, paving the way for genuine healing and growth in the relationship.

In every marriage, disagreements, misunderstandings, and mistakes are inevitable. Sometimes, it's a harsh word spoken in frustration; other times, it might be a larger issue that causes a rift. These moments can create lasting wounds if not approached with care. When we hold on to hurt, it creates a barrier between us and our spouse, making it difficult to fully trust or connect. Resentment, if left to fester, acts like a wall that separates us emotionally, robbing us of the intimacy and closeness we long for. Forgiveness is what breaks down that wall, allowing healing to happen and bringing us back to each other with a renewed sense of love and understanding.

One of the reasons forgiveness is so essential is because it allows both partners to move forward without the weight of past mistakes. When we carry grudges or dwell on old hurts, it not only weighs down our own hearts but also strains the relationship as a whole. Unresolved resentment often resurfaces during new conflicts, compounding the issue and making resolution even harder. By choosing to forgive, we're deciding not to let past wrongs overshadow our present or future. This choice opens the door to a fresh start, where both partners can continue growing and deepening their bond without the shadows of yesterday clouding today.

Forgiveness is also a key part of our own personal growth. When we refuse to forgive, we risk allowing bitterness to take root in our hearts. This bitterness doesn't only harm the marriage—it affects every part of our lives. It can spill over into our relationships with family, friends, and even impact our spiritual journey. By letting go of anger and choosing forgiveness, we free ourselves from the negative weight of resentment. This inner freedom brings peace, allowing us to be fully present in our marriage and more compassionate in our interactions. We find ourselves with a lighter heart, ready to show empathy and kindness to our spouse.

In Christian teachings, forgiveness is more than just a good practice; it's a command from God. Jesus emphasized the importance of forgiveness throughout His ministry, reminding us that we are called to forgive as we have been forgiven. This perspective transforms forgiveness from simply a noble act into a way of life, one that reflects the grace we've received. When couples choose to forgive, they are following Christ's example and building a foundation for their marriage on principles of love, mercy, and grace. Forgiving our spouse is a way of honoring God's call to love one another, even when it's difficult. It allows His love to flow through us and into our relationship, strengthening the bond we share.

Forgiveness creates a safe environment for vulnerability, which is essential in any strong marriage. When forgiveness is practiced, both partners feel secure enough to admit their mistakes without fear of lingering judgment or anger. This sense of safety is vital for open communication and trust. When a spouse knows that forgiveness is possible, that their partner's love doesn't hinge on perfection, they are more likely to be honest, transparent, and committed to working on the relationship. This type of love is unconditional, based not on flawless behavior but on a shared commitment to grow together. It reminds us that we're loved even in our imperfections, which makes it easier to address issues with honesty, knowing that forgiveness and understanding are waiting.

While forgiveness is a vital part of a healthy marriage, it doesn't mean ignoring or excusing hurtful behavior. Forgiveness is not about overlooking wrongdoing; it's about acknowledging the hurt, discussing it openly, and then choosing to release its hold on us. This choice takes strength and commitment, but it is rewarded with a relationship that is stronger and more resilient. True forgiveness doesn't erase the past—it redefines it. It transforms painful memories into lessons of healing, allowing couples to learn from each experience. By choosing to forgive, we invite God to bring redemption and understanding into our relationship, showing that, while challenges will arise, love, grace, and faith are more powerful than any difficulty we face.

Forgiveness also serves as a reminder of our shared humanity. None of us are perfect; we are all capable of making mistakes. When we forgive, we acknowledge our spouse's imperfections while remembering our own. This understanding creates compassion and patience, which are essential for a healthy and lasting marriage. By forgiving, we accept that marriage is not a journey of perfection, but one of growth, understanding, and grace. We learn to see each other through the lens of love, not judgment, and commit to building a relationship that reflects God's unconditional love.

Forgiveness is a gift that brings healing, peace, and a renewed connection. By choosing to let go of past hurts, we open our hearts to a deeper understanding and a love that is resilient and unbreakable. When both partners commit to practicing forgiveness, they create a marriage grounded in compassion, unity, and the enduring grace of God. Through forgiveness, we remind ourselves that we are not alone in this journey. With God's help, we can rise above any challenge, building a marriage that is a true testament to His love.

Practical Steps to True Forgiveness and Letting Go

Forgiveness, especially when the hurt runs deep, can feel like a daunting task. It's often much easier said than done. However, taking practical steps can make the process more achievable, bringing genuine peace and healing to your relationship.

The journey begins by acknowledging the hurt. Forgiveness doesn't mean pretending nothing happened or ignoring painful feelings. Instead, it starts with a willingness to recognize and admit that you've been hurt. Suppressing or denying these emotions can lead to lingering resentment, which only complicates future interactions. Acknowledging the pain doesn't mean dwelling on it; rather, it's about validating your feelings so they can be addressed with honesty and compassion. When we take time to understand why we feel hurt, we can better process those emotions and understand their impact on our relationship.

Once you've recognized your feelings, it's essential to communicate them with your spouse. Honest conversation is the foundation for true healing. Approach this discussion with an open heart, focusing on understanding rather than assigning blame. Using "I" statements, such as "I felt hurt when…," allows you to share your emotions without sounding accusatory. This way, your spouse is more likely to listen without feeling defensive. The goal here is not to revisit the conflict but to express your feelings in a way that invites understanding and empathy.

Just as it's important to share your own feelings, it's equally vital to listen openly to your partner's perspective. Active listening means setting aside your own thoughts and genuinely focusing on what your spouse is sharing. This step often reveals insights that can shift your understanding of the situation, helping you see things from their viewpoint. Listening with empathy builds a bridge of understanding and fosters a space where both partners feel heard and respected.

A crucial part of true forgiveness is accepting responsibility where needed. Sometimes, forgiveness requires looking inward and acknowledging any part we may have played in the situation. This isn't about blaming ourselves but about owning any words or actions that may have contributed to the issue. Taking responsibility shows maturity and a commitment to reconciliation. Often, this willingness can inspire your spouse to reflect on their role as well, leading to mutual understanding and healing.

Forgiveness itself is a conscious choice. It's not merely a feeling that comes naturally but a decision to let go of anger and resentment. This choice may need to be revisited often, especially if feelings of hurt resurface. Reminding yourself of why you chose forgiveness—such as healing the relationship and staying true to your faith—can strengthen your resolve to forgive wholeheartedly.

One of the most challenging steps is releasing resentment. Holding onto anger only deepens the divide between you and your spouse. Letting go doesn't mean forgetting what happened; it means choosing not to let the hurt control your emotions or influence your actions. Releasing these feelings frees both partners from the weight of past conflicts and allows for a fresh start. This decision to let go paves the way for love, compassion, and new beginnings.

Sometimes, reaching a place of forgiveness may feel out of reach on your own. In such cases, seeking support from a trusted pastor, counselor, or mentor can provide guidance. These individuals can offer advice rooted in biblical teachings, helping you work through the emotional process of forgiving. Having someone to share your journey with, whether it's a prayer group or supportive friends, can offer valuable encouragement as you work toward peace.

Forgiveness is also deeply tied to faith, and seeking God's help through prayer can be transformative. Praying for strength, patience, and understanding can shift your heart towards forgiveness. Asking God to help you see your spouse through His eyes can make it easier to release anger and choose compassion. When couples pray together, it not only brings spiritual unity but also reinforces the commitment to overcome challenges with God's guidance and strength.

Forgiveness is a process that often takes time, especially when the hurt is significant. It's essential to be patient with yourself and with your spouse as you navigate this journey. Progress may come in small steps, and that's okay. What matters is the commitment to healing and growth. Celebrate moments of progress and stay willing to keep moving forward, even if setbacks occur. True forgiveness doesn't demand perfection; it only asks for patience and a genuine desire to rebuild trust.

After deciding to forgive, work on replacing lingering negative thoughts with positive ones. Reflect on the good moments you've shared, the qualities you admire in your spouse, and the blessings within your marriage. Focusing on gratitude can shift your mindset and strengthen your choice to forgive. It's a gentle reminder that, while conflicts are part of every relationship, the love and memories you share are the foundation worth nurturing.

Forgiveness isn't just about letting go of the past; it's about committing to a future that prioritizes love, understanding, and growth. This commitment means choosing to avoid bringing up old conflicts in new disagreements and focusing on solutions rather than dwelling on past problems. Trust may take time to rebuild, but with steady effort, it can be restored and even strengthened.

True forgiveness is a continuous journey that deepens a marriage over time. It requires intentional effort, faith, and a willingness to grow together. When both partners embrace forgiveness as a core practice, their marriage becomes grounded in compassion and resilience, reflecting the love and teachings of Christ in daily life.

Scripture Focus: Embracing Forgiveness in Marriage (Matthew 6:14-15, Colossians 3:13)

Forgiveness is central to Christian teachings, and its significance in marriage is profound. Within a marriage, the act of forgiving holds the power to mend, restore, and strengthen the bond between partners, keeping the relationship rooted in faith and grace. The Bible emphasizes forgiveness not just as a practice but as a necessary path toward spiritual growth and relational health. Two key passages—Matthew 6:14-15 and Colossians 3:13—shed light on why forgiveness is so essential and how it can be practiced in a way that reflects God's love.

In Matthew 6:14-15, Jesus teaches, "For if you forgive other people when they sin against you, your heavenly Father will also forgive you. But if you do not forgive others their sins, your Father will not forgive your sins" (NIV). These words from Jesus serve as a powerful reminder of the reciprocal nature of forgiveness. He makes it clear that our willingness to forgive others impacts our own relationship with God. Within marriage, this teaching carries deep meaning. Holding onto grudges or refusing to forgive creates barriers—not only between spouses but also between ourselves and God.

When we forgive, we mirror God's grace in our own lives. In the context of marriage, forgiveness becomes an ongoing commitment, a choice to reflect God's mercy and love daily. This means letting go of past mistakes and offering our spouse the same unconditional grace that God continually offers us. Through this practice, the spiritual bond between husband and wife is strengthened, aligning the relationship more closely with Christ's teachings. It's an act that nurtures both the relationship with one's partner and with God.

Forgiveness is seldom easy, especially when the hurt runs deep. However, recalling God's boundless forgiveness of our own shortcomings can soften our hearts, encouraging us to extend that same grace to our spouse. Jesus's words in Matthew remind us that forgiveness isn't just a one-time action but a way of life. When we choose to forgive, we are living out our faith, fostering spiritual harmony in our marriage and our relationship with God. This passage is both comforting and challenging, calling us to forgive as a testament of our faith and our love.

Another profound insight on forgiveness comes from Colossians 3:13, which instructs, **"Bear with each other and forgive one another if any of you has a grievance against someone. Forgive as the Lord forgave you" (NIV).** Here, the apostle Paul reminds us of the importance of patience and compassion, two essential elements of forgiveness. The phrase "bear with each other" speaks to the reality that relationships require resilience—a willingness to stand by each other, even during difficult times. This call to "forgive as the Lord forgave you" sets a high standard. God's forgiveness is not conditional; it is given freely, fully, and with love. Emulating this level of forgiveness in marriage involves choosing to love and accept our spouse, even in moments of imperfection or conflict.

Colossians 3:13 encourages us to see forgiveness as an act of strength and grace rather than weakness or concession. It's tempting to hold onto anger or resentment, especially when we feel wronged. But the reality is that resentment and anger only breed bitterness, slowly chipping away at the unity and trust within the marriage. When we choose to forgive as God does, we allow healing to take place, restoring what was broken and fortifying the foundation of the relationship.

Incorporating the principles of Colossians 3:13 into daily life can transform how we approach marital conflicts. This scripture calls us to acknowledge and address the hurt but then choose to let it go, releasing its hold on our hearts. Forgiveness, in this sense, is not about denying pain or sweeping issues under the rug. It's about facing the hurt, understanding it, and then intentionally releasing it. This approach prevents unresolved issues from accumulating and promotes a continuous cycle of healing and renewal in the relationship, creating a peaceful and loving environment.

Together, Matthew 6:14-15 and Colossians 3:13 reveal that forgiveness is both a divine command and a path toward deeper love and connection. Embracing forgiveness in marriage aligns the relationship with God's principles, creating a sanctuary where both partners can grow spiritually and emotionally. When forgiveness is guided by scripture, it becomes a powerful force that strengthens marriage, making it a true reflection of God's boundless grace and love.

Prayers for Seeking and Offering Forgiveness

Prayer is a powerful way to connect with God, bringing peace and clarity to moments that may feel heavy with hurt or misunderstanding. In marriage, seeking and offering forgiveness can be challenging, especially when emotions run deep. But prayer can serve as the bridge, linking our hearts to God's wisdom and giving us the strength and humility needed to forgive or ask for forgiveness. When we invite God into our journey of forgiveness, we allow Him to guide the healing process, reinforcing the bond between us and our spouse.

Prayer for Seeking Forgiveness

Heavenly Father, I come before You with a heart that longs for peace and understanding. I recognize my imperfections and the ways I may have caused pain. I ask for Your grace and strength to admit my wrongs and seek forgiveness from my spouse. Help me approach this moment with humility and honesty, free from pride or defensiveness. Give me the words to express my regret sincerely and the courage to receive the response with patience. Lord, fill my heart with compassion so that this moment brings healing rather than distance. Thank You for Your endless love and for teaching me the power of forgiveness. Amen.

Prayer for Offering Forgiveness

Dear Lord, You know the hurt I carry in my heart. I bring this pain to You and ask for the strength to forgive, just as You have forgiven me. Help me to release anger, resentment, and bitterness so that I may walk in peace and love. Let me see my spouse through Your eyes—with compassion, understanding, and grace. Remind me that forgiveness is not only for the one I forgive but also for my own peace and the strength of our shared journey. Thank You for guiding me, filling my heart with

Your love, and showing me how to extend that love to my spouse. I trust in Your healing power to restore what has been broken. Amen.

Joint Prayer for Healing and Unity

Lord, we come before You as one, seeking Your guidance and healing in our relationship. We acknowledge our struggles and ask for Your presence as we journey toward forgiveness. Help us to communicate with honesty, respect, and love. Show us how to forgive each other fully, just as You have forgiven us. May Your peace fill our hearts, replacing any lingering hurt with hope and joy. Strengthen our bond, Lord, so we can move forward together, more united than before. We thank You for being our comfort and for teaching us that, with You, all things are possible. Amen.

Prayer for Long-Term Healing and Growth

Father God, as we continue on this journey of marriage, we ask that You help us maintain a spirit of forgiveness. Teach us to release past grievances and focus on the love and commitment that brought us together. Remind us that each day is an opportunity for growth, and that Your mercy is renewed every morning. Help us to show each other patience, kindness, and understanding in all circumstances. When challenges arise, may we seek You first and let Your wisdom guide our words and actions. Thank You for being our steady support and for blessing our union. Amen.

Daily Prayer for Grace and Understanding

Lord, we thank You for the gift of our marriage and the journey we share. We know each day may bring its own challenges, but we trust that Your grace is sufficient for us. Help us to be quick to forgive and slow to anger. Let our home be filled with Your peace, and teach us to handle conflicts with love and patience. Guide our conversations so that they reflect Your teachings and bring us closer together. We trust in Your love to guide us and keep us grounded in faith. Amen.

Include prayer into your journey toward forgiveness opens the door to peace and healing. Whether you're seeking forgiveness, offering it, or praying together as a couple, these moments with God can reshape your approach to conflict and deepen the love between you.

Chapter 4

Conflict Resolution Strategies Rooted in Faith
Creating a Safe Environment for Discussions

Creating a safe environment for open discussions is foundational in resolving conflicts within a marriage. This safe space is where both partners can share their feelings and thoughts freely, without fear of judgment or backlash. It's a space where each person feels valued, heard, and respected, even when there are disagreements. For Christian couples, creating this type of environment reflects Christ's teachings of love, patience, and understanding, becoming an expression of their faith.

Building a safe space begins with mutual respect. Both spouses need to agree that their goal in any discussion is to understand each other, not to win an argument. This shared commitment helps create trust. When each partner commits to being respectful and kind, they lay the groundwork for a meaningful, loving conversation where both voices are honored.

Listening without interruption is another vital part of a safe environment. Allowing your spouse to speak without cutting in shows respect and signals that you genuinely care about what they're sharing. Practicing active listening—making eye contact, nodding, and using gentle prompts like "I understand" or "Please, go on"—shows that you're fully present. These small actions demonstrate that you're tuned in, helping your spouse feel genuinely valued and understood.

Another way to foster a safe space is to remove distractions. Turn off the TV, put away your phones, and find a quiet place to talk. When your focus is entirely on each other, it creates an atmosphere where both of you feel honored and heard. Setting aside dedicated time and space for tough discussions signals that your relationship is a priority, even when life is busy.

Tone of voice and body language are also key in creating a sense of safety. A calm, warm tone conveys care, while crossed arms or a tense expression can feel defensive, even if the words themselves are neutral.

Practicing open body language—keeping arms relaxed, maintaining eye contact, and sitting comfortably—helps create a welcoming space for honest dialogue. This openness encourages vulnerability and makes it easier to communicate from the heart.

Setting some simple ground rules can further enhance safety in discussions. These rules could include a commitment to avoid accusations, refraining from raising voices, and steering clear of past grievances during the conversation. Ground rules act as a framework that both partners can rely on to keep the conversation respectful and focused. This structure can make it easier to handle sensitive issues without escalation.

Beginning with prayer is another powerful way to create a safe environment. Praying together invites God's presence into the conversation and reminds both partners of their shared faith and commitment. A simple prayer for wisdom, patience, and understanding can shift the atmosphere, helping to calm nerves and soften hearts. By bringing God into the conversation, couples reinforce their intention to work together with His guidance, strengthening their bond.

Creating a safe space for discussions may take practice, but with consistency, it can become a natural part of how you communicate. When both partners feel secure, they're more likely to speak openly, which leads to a deeper understanding and a more resilient relationship. This foundation of respect, love, and faith fosters a marriage where conflicts are approached not as opposing forces but as a unified team, each partner supporting and learning from the other.

Step-by-Step Conflict Resolution Process

Resolving conflicts in marriage goes beyond voicing frustrations; it requires a thoughtful, structured approach that leads to genuine understanding and healing. This step-by-step process offers a clear path for handling disagreements constructively, helping both partners feel respected, valued, and heard. When used with patience and faith, these steps turn conflict into a chance for deeper connection and growth.

Step 1: Identify the Issue Clearly and Calmly

Start by defining the problem without assigning blame. Approach the conversation with a focus on solutions rather than placing fault. Instead of saying, "You never help with chores," try, "I feel overwhelmed when tasks pile up, and I could use some help." This reframing allows you to share your needs without making your spouse feel attacked. A clear, calm tone from the beginning helps set a constructive mood for the conversation.

Step 2: Listen to Understand, Not Just to Respond

Once the issue is defined, allow each partner time to share their perspective fully. When it's your turn to listen, set aside your own thoughts and focus on understanding what your spouse is saying. Maintain eye contact, nod to show engagement, and avoid interrupting. Reflecting back what you've heard, like saying, "I hear you saying that…" or "So, you're feeling…," can confirm that you understand. This creates a space where both partners feel truly heard, even if you don't entirely agree.

Step 3: Validate Each Other's Feelings

Validation doesn't mean you have to agree with everything; it simply means acknowledging that your spouse's feelings are real and important to them. Phrases like, "I understand why you feel that way," or "I see how this affects you," convey empathy and care. This step builds trust, showing that both voices matter and that feelings are respected.

Step 4: Focus on Shared Goals and Interests

Resolving conflict becomes easier when both partners look for common ground rather than focusing on differences. Identify what both of you ultimately want from the situation. For instance, if the issue is financial, maybe both of you are aiming for financial stability but have different ways of getting there. Recognizing shared goals turns the conversation from "me versus you" into "us working together." This approach encourages teamwork and cooperation.

Step 5: Brainstorm Solutions Together

With the issue clear and shared goals in mind, work together to come up with potential solutions. This step involves flexibility and a willingness to compromise. Allow each other to suggest ideas without judgment or criticism. Not every idea will work, but the goal is to explore possibilities without shutting each other down. A spirit of openness fosters creativity and can lead to solutions that feel fair to both of you.

Step 6: Agree on a Plan of Action

After discussing solutions, decide on a specific, realistic plan. Make sure both partners feel comfortable with it and that the details are clear to avoid future misunderstandings. For instance, if you decide to split household tasks, agree on a fair division and set a date to review how it's going. Setting expectations and timelines prevents the issue from resurfacing and helps both partners feel assured.

Step 7: Pray for Guidance and Strength

Praying together after reaching a resolution can reinforce your agreement and bring peace into the process. Ask for God's guidance, patience, and strength to uphold the choices you've made and handle future conflicts with grace. Prayer not only strengthens your bond but reminds you that your relationship is grounded in shared faith and purpose.

Step 8: Practice Accountability

Following through on the agreed plan is essential to building trust. Each partner should hold themselves accountable for their part in the solution, making an effort to fulfill the commitment made during the discussion. Accountability helps ensure that conflicts don't repeat and that each partner feels respected and supported.

Step 9: Reflect and Adjust as Needed

Over time, you may need to make adjustments to the solution based on what works best for your relationship. Be open to discussing changes if something isn't working as expected. Regular check-ins to see how things are going show that both partners are committed to growth and willing to adapt for the good of the relationship. Flexibility helps you both stay aligned and maintain harmony over time.

By following these steps, you and your spouse can approach disagreements with patience, compassion, and faith. This process promotes open communication, reinforces mutual respect, and lays a foundation of trust and understanding that grows stronger with each challenge.

Examples of How to Navigate Tough Conversations

Tough conversations are a normal part of any marriage. Learning how to approach these moments with love and respect can make all the difference in maintaining harmony and understanding. Below are examples of how couples can navigate difficult discussions, keeping unity at the heart of each exchange.

Example 1: Discussing Financial Concerns

Money is often a sensitive subject in marriage, especially when partners have different views on spending or saving. Imagine a situation where one spouse feels uneasy about their budget, while the other wants to make a significant purchase. Here's how they could handle this conversation constructively:

a. **Express Concerns Without Blame**: Instead of saying, "You're always spending too much," one spouse might start with, "I'm feeling a bit anxious about our finances and would love to go over our budget together." This approach opens the door for dialogue without triggering defensiveness.

b. **Listen to Each Other's Perspectives**: The other spouse might respond, "I understand your concern. I feel like this purchase would really improve our quality of life, but I'm open to talking about ways to fit it into our budget."

c. **Find a Compromise**: Together, they brainstorm solutions, like saving a small amount each month toward the purchase or finding a similar but more affordable option. They also agree to check in regularly on their budget to ensure they're meeting their goals together.

d. **Pray for Guidance**: After reaching an understanding, they take a moment to pray together, asking for wisdom and stewardship over their finances, trusting that God will guide them toward decisions that honor their marriage and future.

This approach keeps honesty, patience, and teamwork front and center, helping turn what could be a divisive conversation into a shared effort toward a common goal.

Example 2: Addressing Differences in Parenting Styles

Parenting is a deeply personal journey, and each parent brings their own experiences and beliefs to the table. Suppose one parent believes in firm discipline while the other prefers a more relaxed approach. Here's how they might approach this delicate subject:

a. **Acknowledge the Issue**: One spouse might say, "I've noticed we handle discipline differently, and I think it's affecting the consistency we show the kids. Can we talk about how to find some middle ground?"

b. **Share Perspectives with Openness**: Both partners take turns sharing their views without judgment. For example, one might say, "I think setting clear rules gives structure," while the other could respond, "I feel that being a bit more flexible helps the kids develop independence."

c. **Identify Shared Values**: They both agree on core values they want to instill in their children—values like respect, kindness, and responsibility. With these shared goals in mind, they can work together to find a balance.

d. **Agree on a Plan**: They decide on a set of core rules that both will follow while allowing flexibility in less critical areas. They also agree to review their approach regularly to ensure it's working for their family.

e. **Pray for Unity in Parenting**: They pray together, seeking God's guidance in raising their children. This shared prayer reinforces their commitment to parenting as a united team, grounded in love and faith.

By approaching this conversation with open minds and hearts, they can avoid a power struggle and instead create a balanced approach that respects both their perspectives.

Example 3: Resolving Tensions Around Family Boundaries

Boundaries with extended family can sometimes be a sensitive topic, especially if one partner values close family ties while the other feels overwhelmed by frequent visits. Here's how they could approach this conversation with care:

a. **Start with Understanding**: The spouse feeling overwhelmed might say, "I love your family and appreciate how close they are to us, but I sometimes feel stressed by how often they visit. Could we talk about finding a balance that works for both of us?"

b. **Share Each Partner's Feelings**: The other spouse might respond, "Family has always been a big part of my life, and I feel connected when we spend time together. But I also want you to feel at ease in our home."

c. **Brainstorm Solutions Together**: They discuss various options, such as designating specific days for family visits or hosting family gatherings in other locations. This allows them to respect both the need for personal space and the value of family bonds.

d. **Agree and Adjust Over Time**: They decide to try this new approach and agree to check in after a month to see how they're both feeling. They commit to revisiting the conversation as needed, staying flexible and open to each other's needs.

e. **Pray for Guidance and Peace**: Praying together for wisdom and harmony can help bring a sense of peace, trusting that God will guide them in finding a balance that honors both their marriage and their families.

Example 4: The Problem of Money in Marriage

Money is one of the most common sources of conflict in marriage. Differences in spending, saving, or budgeting can quickly lead to misunderstandings and tension. Suppose one spouse is more financially cautious, focusing on saving for the future, while the other prefers to spend on immediate comforts or family experiences. Here's how they might approach this conversation to foster understanding:

a. **Express Concerns Openly, Without Accusation**: One spouse might begin by saying, "I sometimes worry about our future finances, and I'd love to discuss how we can both feel secure and comfortable with our budget." Starting with "I" statements and focusing on shared goals helps avoid triggering defensiveness.

b. **Listen to Understand Each Other's Priorities**: The other spouse might respond with, "I appreciate your concerns. I feel that spending on family experiences enriches our lives, but I'm open to finding a balance that works for both of us." This mutual understanding acknowledges each other's values around money.

c. **Agree on a Financial Plan Together**: The couple can work together to create a budget that reflects both priorities. They might agree to set aside a specific amount for savings each month, along with a portion for enjoying life now. Reviewing this plan regularly can help them stay aligned as their financial goals evolve.

d. **Seek God's Wisdom in Prayer**: Inviting God into the conversation through prayer can bring clarity and peace. Together, they can pray for guidance to be good stewards of their finances, trusting that God will provide for their needs.

This approach helps couples tackle financial challenges as a team, turning what could be a source of division into an opportunity for unity.

Example 5: The Problem of Unfaithfulness in Relationships

Infidelity is one of the most painful challenges a marriage can face. When trust is broken, it takes patience, honesty, and commitment to rebuild. Suppose one partner has been unfaithful, and both spouses are committed to healing their relationship. Here's how they might begin the journey toward restoration:

a. **Begin with a Genuine Apology and Expression of Remorse**: The unfaithful partner should take responsibility for their actions, expressing true regret and empathy for the pain caused. This might sound like, "I know my actions have hurt you deeply, and I am truly sorry. I am committed to earning back your trust."

b. **Create a Safe Space for the Hurt Partner's Feelings**: The partner who has been hurt needs space to express their feelings of anger, betrayal, or sadness without fear of judgment. The unfaithful partner should listen with patience, acknowledging the pain they've caused and refraining from defending themselves.

c. **Commit to Counseling or Professional Help**: Working with a Christian counselor or pastor can provide guidance and accountability during the healing process. Professional support offers a structured path toward understanding the root causes of the infidelity and how to rebuild trust.

d. **Seek Spiritual Healing Through Prayer and Scripture**: Both partners can invite God into their journey of healing, seeking His strength, grace, and wisdom. Praying together and individually can help soften hearts and bring comfort, reminding them that forgiveness and redemption are possible through faith.

Infidelity is a complex issue that requires time and support, but with a commitment to honesty, patience, and God's guidance, couples can find healing and renewal.

Example 6: The Problem of Extended Family in Marriage

Navigating relationships with in-laws and extended family can sometimes put a strain on marriage, especially when boundaries feel unclear. Suppose one spouse feels overwhelmed by the frequency of family gatherings, while the other values close family ties. Here's how they can approach this delicate issue:

a. **Start with Understanding and Compassion**: The concerned spouse might begin by saying, "I love your family and enjoy spending time with them, but sometimes I feel overwhelmed by how often we gather. Could we talk about finding a balance?"

b. **Share Both Perspectives**: The spouse who values family time might respond, "Family has always been important to me, and I feel connected when we spend time together. But I also want to make sure you're comfortable." This exchange creates an atmosphere of empathy and shows that both perspectives are valued.

c. **Agree on Healthy Boundaries Together**: The couple can discuss options, such as designating specific times for family gatherings or hosting gatherings in neutral settings. They might also agree to revisit these boundaries periodically to ensure they work for both partners.

d. **Pray for Unity and Balance**: Praying together can help bring clarity and peace, as they seek guidance on how to honor both their marriage and their family ties. Asking for God's help in setting healthy boundaries can provide the strength to balance love for extended family with prioritizing their own relationship.

This thoughtful approach enables couples to handle family dynamics with understanding and respect, ensuring that both partners feel valued and supported.

Example 7: The Problem of Sexual Dysfunction in Marriage

Physical intimacy is an important aspect of marriage, but issues related to sexual dysfunction can create emotional distance if not addressed. If one partner struggles with physical intimacy, whether due to medical, emotional, or psychological reasons, it's essential to handle this issue with sensitivity. Here's how they might start a conversation on this delicate topic:

a. **Express Concerns with Sensitivity and Respect:** The partner initiating the conversation might say, "I've noticed we haven't been as close physically, and I want to make sure you feel loved and supported. How can we work through this together?" This compassionate approach shows care and concern without assigning blame.

b. **Listen and Validate Each Other's Experiences:** The partner experiencing challenges with intimacy might explain how they feel, whether it's due to physical discomfort, stress, or other factors. The other spouse should listen openly, offering support and understanding. This exchange strengthens emotional intimacy and reassures both partners that they are a team.

c. **Consider Seeking Professional Help**: Consulting with a Christian counselor, medical professional, or therapist can provide valuable insights and guidance. Addressing the root causes of the issue, whether physical or emotional, can lead to effective solutions that support both partners' well-being.

d. **Pray for Patience and Understanding**: Together, the couple can pray for guidance, patience, and love as they navigate this sensitive area. Inviting God into the healing process can provide comfort and reinforce their commitment to one another.

By addressing intimacy issues with sensitivity and support, couples can overcome these challenges together, building a deeper connection that honors both emotional and physical closeness.

Navigating sensitive issues with understanding and patience helps ensure that both partners feel respected and valued. These examples show that tough conversations, when approached with thoughtfulness and care, can lead to greater connection and a stronger foundation for your marriage.

Action Points – Steps to Apply After Conflict Resolution

After resolving a conflict, it's natural to feel a sense of relief and even accomplishment. But true, lasting change takes time, patience, and a commitment to growth. It's essential to give both yourself and your spouse grace as you work toward these changes together—understanding that nothing shifts overnight. These action points provide practical steps for reinforcing the resolutions you've made, helping ensure that each agreement becomes part of the relationship's foundation. Here's how to carry the understanding from the discussion forward in a meaningful way.

1. Reflect on the Conversation

Take a few moments individually to think about what was discussed. Reflecting allows each person to absorb the conversation, recognizing areas of growth and affirming the positive steps taken. It's a chance to appreciate what went well and identify any personal adjustments needed. Embrace this time as a personal check-in to acknowledge progress and commit to continued openness in the relationship.

2. Express Appreciation

Show gratitude to your spouse for their willingness to address the issue and work through it with you. Even a simple "Thank you for listening" or "I appreciate how we talked through that together" fosters warmth and respect, reinforcing your shared commitment to growth. Expressing appreciation deepens trust and makes future conversations more approachable.

3. Review the Agreed-Upon Plan

Revisit the solution you reached together, ensuring that both of you are clear on the steps moving forward. This brief review helps prevent misunderstandings and strengthens your joint commitment to change. Clarifying any details now will reduce potential for confusion, and create a sense of unity around the chosen path forward.

4. Implement the Plan with Consistency

Consistency is essential in transforming a resolution into a lasting change. Both partners need to actively participate in maintaining the agreed actions, whether it's shifting a habit, adjusting routines, or dividing responsibilities differently. Making an effort to consistently uphold your commitments shows mutual respect and dedication. It's in these steady, small steps that lasting change truly takes root.

5. Give Yourselves Time and Patience

Change takes time, and no plan is perfect from the start. Extend grace to yourselves as you navigate this process. There might be moments of frustration or setbacks along the way, but patience is a key part of growth. Remember, growth doesn't happen overnight, and learning from the journey itself can be as valuable as reaching the destination. Letting go of the pressure for immediate perfection allows each partner to feel supported and encourages persistence.

6. Set a Check-In Date

Decide on a time to revisit the topic, whether that's in a week, a month, or another suitable timeframe. Scheduling a check-in offers a chance to celebrate progress, adjust the plan as needed, and reinforce your commitment to each other. Knowing that there will be an opportunity to discuss the issue again removes any pressure to make everything perfect right away.

7. Practice Forgiveness and Release the Past

After reaching a resolution, choose to let go of any remaining resentment or hurt. Holding onto past grievances can create tension even after an issue is supposedly resolved. Actively practicing forgiveness—both for yourself and for your spouse—creates a healthier space for growth. Releasing past hurts allows both partners to embrace a fresh outlook, free from lingering negativity.

8. Encourage Each Other

Provide gentle support as you both work on the agreed solution, especially if it involves creating new habits or approaches. A simple "Thank you for doing that" or "I noticed you made an effort with…" can make a significant impact. Encouragement shows your appreciation for your spouse's commitment, reinforcing the idea that each of you values the other's growth.

9. Pray for Guidance and Strength

Prayer can be a source of strength and unity as you work toward lasting change. Ask God to give you wisdom, patience, and guidance, both individually and as a couple. Praying together keeps your relationship grounded in faith and reminds both partners that their strength ultimately comes from God. Seeking His help can make the process of change feel more achievable and bring peace during challenging moments.

10. Celebrate Small Wins Along the Way

Acknowledge every small step forward—whether it's a productive conversation, an improvement in daily routines, or simply a stronger feeling of connection. Celebrating these small victories keeps you motivated and reinforces that progress is being made. It's a reminder that every step counts and that both partners are committed to building a stronger marriage, one day at a time.

11. Keep the Lines of Communication Open

Finally, make it a priority to keep communication open and honest moving forward. Agree that it's okay to revisit any concerns if they arise again and that your relationship is a safe place for expressing thoughts and feelings. By maintaining a proactive approach, you prevent issues from building up and ensure that each partner feels valued and heard.

By applying these action points, resolutions become part of the fabric of your relationship, creating a foundation for a marriage that is resilient, respectful, and loving. Remember, progress often comes in small, steady steps. Through patience, encouragement, and a shared commitment, each step you take together builds a marriage that is equipped to face future challenges with faith and unity.

Chapter 5

Daily Practices for a Healthy, Conflict-Free Marriage

Building Habits That Encourage Understanding and Peace

In marriage, building habits that nurture understanding and peace forms a solid foundation for a lasting, loving relationship. Daily practices like gratitude, quality time, empathy, prayer, kindness, and forgiveness create an atmosphere where love flourishes and minor conflicts don't take root. Here's how each of these habits can become a cornerstone in your marriage.

Gratitude

Expressing gratitude regularly brings positivity into the relationship. When you take a moment to acknowledge a kind act or express thanks, you're creating a cycle of appreciation that encourages joy. Gratitude shifts your focus away from any imperfections and highlights the good, reinforcing a sense of satisfaction and peace. Simple words like "Thank you for helping with dinner" or "I appreciate your support" show your spouse they're valued. Small acts of appreciation can transform the everyday moments into reminders of love, helping to maintain a positive outlook even when challenges arise.

Spending Quality Time Together

Life can be demanding, but setting aside meaningful moments together strengthens connection. Quality time doesn't need to be elaborate; sometimes, it's about savoring a quiet breakfast or taking a walk after dinner. These shared moments allow you to unwind and refocus on each other, deepening intimacy and creating a rhythm of companionship. By making time for each other daily, you nurture a sense of closeness and unity. Over time, this simple practice can build a reservoir of shared memories, helping the relationship stay resilient and joyful.

Practicing Empathy

Empathy, or seeing things from your spouse's perspective, transforms interactions. During times of stress or misunderstanding, empathy helps you respond with patience and compassion. Pausing to consider your partner's feelings creates an environment of mutual respect and understanding, easing communication even in tense moments. Practicing empathy daily—whether by listening attentively or pausing before responding—reinforces that both partners are valued and heard. When empathy becomes a habit, it fosters a home where grace and patience are naturally extended, making challenges easier to navigate together.

Praying Together

Prayer deepens the spiritual foundation of marriage, bringing partners closer to each other and to God. Daily prayer reminds couples that their relationship is part of a greater purpose, rooted in faith. By praying together, you're inviting God's presence into your relationship, strengthening the bond through shared faith. Prayer can be a moment of gratitude in the morning or asking for strength at night, uniting you in a shared spiritual journey. This practice not only provides comfort but also aligns your hearts with God's guidance, reinforcing your commitment to each other and your shared beliefs.

Acts of Kindness

Small acts of kindness create a culture of love and respect in marriage. A thoughtful note, a favorite snack, or a small gesture of help communicates care. When kindness becomes a regular part of your relationship, it fosters an atmosphere where both partners feel cherished. These daily acts don't need to be grand; they just need to be heartfelt. Over time, kindness diffuses tension, nurtures affection, and reinforces the idea that each partner is dedicated to the other's well-being, making the relationship a safe and happy place to be.

Expressing Forgiveness

Daily forgiveness prevents small issues from accumulating into larger conflicts. When you make it a habit to release minor frustrations or let go of small misunderstandings, you're ensuring that the relationship remains free of unnecessary tension. A simple "It's okay" or "Let's move forward" can be all it takes to clear the air, allowing both partners to engage with each other in peace. Daily forgiveness doesn't mean ignoring real issues, but it does mean addressing minor frustrations with grace, creating a space where both partners feel valued and understood. This habit allows each day to start fresh, keeping past grievances from clouding the relationship.

By integrating these habits into daily life, couples lay a foundation of trust, love, and peace that supports a strong and lasting marriage. These practices build a culture of mutual respect and support, nurturing a bond that grows deeper over time. Through gratitude, time together, empathy, prayer, kindness, and forgiveness, each partner invests in a relationship that can withstand challenges and flourish in faith and love.

Weekly Check-Ins and How to Make Them Meaningful

Weekly check-ins are an invaluable tool for strengthening a marriage, providing a dedicated time to touch base on what's going well and what might need some attention. These regular moments create a rhythm of open communication and mutual support, fostering closeness, trust, and a proactive approach to handling minor issues before they grow.

Choosing a consistent time and place is key to making these check-ins meaningful. Pick a moment when you can both be comfortable and free from distractions, like a Saturday morning over coffee, a Sunday evening walk, or a quiet moment after the kids are in bed. The goal is to find a regular time that fits your routine, ensuring you're both fully present and committed. By establishing this rhythm, you're showing each other that this connection matters.

Start each check-in on a positive note. Expressing gratitude or acknowledging something your spouse did well during the week creates an encouraging atmosphere. You might say, "I really appreciated how you helped with dinner," or "Thank you for being so supportive." These simple affirmations set a warm tone, making both partners feel valued and appreciated from the beginning.

Discussing what's going well in the relationship is another way to reinforce positivity. Celebrate small victories, improvements, or simply appreciate each other. Recognizing these moments helps both of you see the strength in your relationship and reinforces the habits that bring you closer. This focus on the good creates a foundation of shared commitment, reminding you both of the joy and value of your partnership.

Check-ins are also a safe space to address areas that need a little attention. Approach this part with honesty and sensitivity, using "I" statements to express feelings without placing blame. For example, you might say, "I felt a bit distant this week when we didn't get much time together." This language encourages open dialogue without making the other person feel defensive. By bringing up these topics weekly, you can handle minor concerns as they come up, preventing them from building into larger issues.

Take a moment to set realistic goals for the coming week. These could be related to spending more quality time, improving communication, or offering more support. For instance, you might decide to plan a date night, pray together each evening, or make time for a shared hobby. These small goals create a sense of teamwork, showing that both partners are actively investing in the marriage.

Ending the check-in with a joint prayer can be a meaningful way to close the conversation. Ask for God's guidance in the areas you've discussed and strength to work on the goals you've set. This moment of spiritual unity reinforces the shared commitment to keeping Christ at the center of your marriage. It also invites God's wisdom and peace into your relationship, helping you approach the coming week with renewed focus and love.

Keep the atmosphere light and comfortable, ensuring that the conversation feels like a bonding moment rather than a chore. When check-ins are natural and enjoyable, both partners look forward to them, knowing they're an opportunity for growth and connection.

Weekly check-ins are a structured but gentle way to stay in tune with each other's needs and experiences. They encourage openness, prevent minor issues from growing into bigger ones, and create a positive cycle of continuous improvement. By making these check-ins a regular part of your marriage, you foster a relationship where love, understanding, and support are nurtured week by week.

Incorporating Shared Devotionals to Reinforce Unity

Including shared devotionals in your marriage is a meaningful way to connect spiritually and deepen your bond. Devotionals offer a regular opportunity for couples to explore their faith together, inviting God's wisdom and guidance into their relationship. This practice reinforces unity and helps both partners align with biblical principles in their daily lives.

The first step in adding devotionals to your routine is finding one that resonates with both of you. Many devotionals focus on marriage, covering topics like love, forgiveness, patience, and communication, while others may offer broader spiritual insights that encourage growth. Take the time to select a devotional that feels relevant to your journey as a couple. Whether you prefer daily readings or a more in-depth weekly study, the key is choosing material that both of you find inspiring and meaningful.

Consistency is important for making shared devotionals a lasting part of your relationship. Decide on a time that fits your schedule, whether it's in the morning to start your day or in the evening to wind down together. If daily devotionals feel overwhelming, try once or twice a week. Creating a regular routine gives you both something to look forward to, making it a cherished part of your schedule.

After reading or listening to a devotional, take a few moments to share your thoughts and reflections. Discuss what resonated with you, how the message applies to your marriage, or any insights that stood out. This open dialogue encourages honesty and allows both of you to understand each other's thoughts and challenges more deeply. For example, if the devotional discusses patience, one of you might share how you're working on being more patient, while the other offers encouragement. These conversations create a safe space for spiritual growth and strengthen your emotional connection.

One of the most powerful aspects of shared devotionals is the opportunity to put the lessons into practice. As you read, think about how the devotional's message can shape your actions, attitudes, and decisions. If the topic is kindness, you might commit to showing small acts of kindness toward each other. If it's forgiveness, you could take a moment to release any lingering resentment. These practical applications bring the words to life, allowing both of you to live out your faith in ways that enrich your relationship.

After reflecting, close the devotional time with a prayer. Thank God for the insights you've gained and ask for His help in applying them to your marriage. Praying together reinforces your commitment to spiritual growth and reminds you both that you are united in faith. A simple prayer of gratitude or a request for guidance provides peace and strength for the days ahead.

While consistency is valuable, it's also essential to remain flexible. Life can get busy, and there may be weeks when finding time for a devotional is more challenging. If you miss a day or need to adjust your schedule, remember that devotionals are meant to bring joy and connection, not stress. Allow yourselves grace and focus on making the most of the times you do share, knowing that each moment spent together in God's word is meaningful.

Some devotional topics may feel especially impactful or challenging, and it's okay to revisit these as needed. If a passage or message resonates deeply, consider reading it again or discussing it further. Revisiting certain devotionals can reinforce important lessons, offering new insights as you grow together. This approach allows you both to reflect more deeply on areas that need extra attention, supporting a marriage grounded in intentional, faith-based growth.

Incorporating shared devotionals creates a foundation of faith that brings you closer as a couple. This practice strengthens not only your spiritual connection but also the emotional and practical aspects of your relationship. As you explore devotionals together, you build a marriage centered on God, aligned with His teachings, and filled with mutual respect and understanding.

Quick Tips – Simple Daily Actions to Build Marital Strength

Building a resilient and joyful marriage doesn't always require grand gestures or lengthy conversations. Often, it's the small, everyday actions that build lasting strength in a relationship. By incorporating simple habits into your daily life, you create a foundation of love, respect, and understanding that supports both partners through life's ups and downs.

Starting and ending the day with affection is a powerful way to set a positive tone. A warm greeting in the morning or a loving goodbye at night reminds each other of your affection. Whether it's a hug, a kiss, or a kind word, these small moments keep your connection strong and help both partners feel loved and valued.

Another simple but impactful gesture is sending small messages of appreciation. A quick text or a note expressing gratitude or admiration can make a big difference, especially on busy days. Even a short message like "I appreciate you" or "Thinking of you" shows your spouse that they're in your thoughts and that their efforts are noticed.

Encouraging each other is essential, whether your spouse is facing a challenge at work or pursuing a personal goal. Simple words like "I believe in you" or "You've got this" remind them that they have a partner by their side. Offering encouragement strengthens the relationship by building confidence and showing that both partners are invested in each other's happiness.

Active listening is another daily habit that goes a long way in strengthening a marriage. Taking the time to truly listen, even in casual conversations, shows respect and helps prevent misunderstandings. Active listening means giving full attention, avoiding interruptions, and responding thoughtfully, helping your spouse feel valued and understood.

Expressing forgiveness quickly can prevent minor irritations from building up. Letting go of small annoyances or offering forgiveness promptly with a simple "It's okay" or "Let's move on" keeps the atmosphere light. Quick forgiveness promotes a peaceful environment, where both partners feel free from lingering tension.

Sharing laughter brings joy and ease to the relationship. Whether it's sharing a joke, watching a funny show together, or reminiscing about happy memories, laughter reminds both partners to enjoy each other's company. Humor is a powerful way to keep the relationship vibrant and connected.

Acts of kindness—like making your spouse's favorite breakfast or tackling a chore they dislike—show thoughtfulness and care. These small gestures reinforce love and respect, creating an atmosphere of mutual appreciation. Kindness, even in small doses, strengthens the bond and keeps the relationship warm.

Praying together, even briefly, is another way to reinforce unity. A quick prayer for guidance or gratitude each day centers your marriage in faith and helps both partners feel connected to God and each other. These short moments of shared faith provide comfort and encouragement, especially during challenging times.

Complimenting each other regularly helps build self-esteem and shows admiration. Simple compliments, like "You did a great job" or "You look wonderful today," remind your spouse that they are cherished. Regular compliments foster a culture of respect and appreciation in the relationship.

Checking in about each other's day creates a sense of partnership. This doesn't have to be an in-depth conversation; a simple question about their day shows interest in their experiences and keeps both partners engaged in each other's lives.

Sharing a distraction-free meal is another way to reconnect. Whether it's breakfast, dinner, or a quick coffee break, eating together without screens or interruptions allows you to enjoy each other's presence. Regular, focused time together strengthens the relationship and makes each partner feel valued.

Celebrating small achievements, like meeting a work deadline or completing a personal project, shows that you're invested in each other's growth and success. Recognizing even minor accomplishments builds positivity and encourages continuous growth.

Setting aside dedicated time for each other helps maintain a vibrant connection. Even just 15 minutes of undistracted time together can be refreshing and bonding, keeping the relationship feeling prioritized despite life's demands.

Reflecting on a Bible verse together provides mutual encouragement and spiritual unity. A short reflection on a meaningful verse brings God's wisdom into your daily lives, aligning your relationship with faith-based principles.

Finally, keeping communication gentle and kind, even in disagreement, ensures that both partners feel safe and respected. Speaking thoughtfully, even when expressing frustration, creates a positive atmosphere for open communication and keeps the relationship strong.

Including these simple actions into your daily life helps you build a marriage that feels secure, joyful, and deeply connected. A strong marriage is rooted in these small, consistent acts of care and attention that remind both partners that they are valued and loved.

Chapter 6

Real-Life Stories and Testimonies of Faith

Marriage is a journey that sometimes leads through seasons of pain, disappointment, and even betrayal. Even the strongest, most committed couples face challenges that can make them feel as though the bond they built together has been broken. Yet, stories of restoration reveal that, with faith, humility, and effort, a marriage can not only survive but come out stronger than before. When a couple leans on God through the most difficult times, they often find that His grace and love can lead them through the darkness to healing and renewal.

One such story is that of Mark and Julia. Their journey of rebuilding trust after infidelity is a testament to the strength of faith, the power of forgiveness, and the resilience of love. Step by step, they rediscovered what it means to grow together, with God's guidance leading them from brokenness to restoration.

Mark and Julia's Story of Rebuilding Trust After Infidelity

Mark and Julia had been married nearly ten years when their marriage reached an unexpected and devastating crossroads. Like many couples, they had their share of ups and downs, always leaning on each other and their faith to navigate life's challenges. Together, they had built a life filled with shared memories and a loving home for their two children. But as the years went by, life became busier, and they slowly began to drift apart.

Julia felt the distance first. Mark's long hours at work and frequent late nights had left their relationship feeling increasingly shallow. Conversations became about schedules and family logistics, rather than hopes or feelings. Julia occasionally brought up her concerns, but Mark often brushed them off, attributing his distraction to work stress. Deep down, she felt uneasy, but she hesitated to push harder, hoping things would improve on their own.

Then, one evening, Julia discovered a message on Mark's phone from a woman he worked with. Although seemingly innocent, the message carried a tone that made her heart sink. When she confronted Mark, he admitted he had developed an emotional connection that had briefly crossed the line into physical intimacy. For Julia, the world seemed to come crashing down. She felt betrayed, hurt, and utterly disillusioned by the man she had trusted most.

A Time for Reflection and Prayer

In the immediate aftermath, Julia couldn't bear to look at Mark. She stayed with her sister, wrestling with her emotions, her anger, and her sadness. Friends and family offered support, with some even suggesting separation. Yet, despite the immense pain, Julia felt a quiet but unshakable pull in her heart, a feeling that perhaps this was not the end of their marriage.

During these lonely days, Julia turned to God for guidance. Psalm 34:18 comforted her: *"The Lord is close to the brokenhearted and saves those who are crushed in spirit."* This verse became her anchor, a reminder that even in her pain, God was near. As she prayed, she felt a gentle stirring of hope that perhaps, just maybe, there was a way forward.

The First Steps Toward Reconciliation

After several days, Julia agreed to meet with Mark at their pastor's office. In this safe, compassionate setting, they could openly share their pain, guilt, and remorse. Mark admitted he had neglected their marriage, letting his attention shift to someone else instead of investing in Julia and their relationship. He expressed deep regret, unsure how to make things right but willing to try if Julia was open to it.

Though forgiveness felt far off, Julia was willing to explore the possibility of healing—on the condition that Mark would be fully transparent and committed to counseling. They began working with a Christian marriage counselor who helped them explore the factors that led to the affair and to rebuild their relationship from the ground up. It wasn't easy; it was a journey that began not with love or affection, but with honesty, accountability, and a commitment to putting in the hard work.

Healing Through Honesty and Transparency

Those first few months of counseling were some of the hardest they had ever faced. Mark had to be fully transparent, answering Julia's questions about the affair honestly, even when it was uncomfortable. With their counselor's guidance, they worked to establish new boundaries, with Mark sharing his schedule and phone access to show his dedication to healing their relationship.

Through these difficult discussions, they practiced daily check-ins where they would share their feelings, concerns, and hopes. While there were many days when Julia felt overwhelmed by pain, she leaned on verses like Matthew 6:14-15, which reminded her of the value of forgiveness. Slowly, day by day, they began to rediscover a connection that had once felt shattered.

Reconnecting Through Prayer and Faith

A pivotal moment in their journey came when they started praying together. At first, it felt forced, even uncomfortable, but gradually, prayer became their shared strength. Together, they prayed each morning and evening, asking God for patience, guidance, and healing. These moments brought a sense of peace and unity that they hadn't felt in years. They began attending church regularly, joined a couples' Bible study, and found support in a community that reminded them of God's grace.

Through prayer, Julia felt a softening of her heart. It wasn't that her pain had disappeared, but she began to see Mark as a flawed person who was genuinely working to rebuild their relationship. For Mark, these moments deepened his commitment to being the husband Julia deserved.

Building a New Foundation of Trust

Rebuilding trust was no small feat, but Mark knew that every action mattered. With every counseling session, every shared conversation, and every gesture of transparency, he worked to prove his commitment. Their counselor suggested setting "trust milestones"—small goals like spending a full day together without discussing the affair or sharing a heartfelt laugh over an old memory. Each small victory built a stronger foundation than they had before.

Over time, Julia found herself gradually able to trust Mark again. It was not a sudden shift but a slow realization that Mark's dedication was genuine. This new trust formed a deeper, more resilient foundation for their relationship.

A New Beginning

After nearly a year of counseling, prayer, and hard work, Mark and Julia emerged from this difficult chapter not as the couple they once were, but as something new. They had faced the unimaginable and found a way through, growing stronger in the process. Their relationship had transformed—built not on past expectations, but on honesty, humility, and shared faith.

Today, Mark and Julia's journey stands as a testament to the power of faith, forgiveness, and intentional love. They share their story with other couples facing difficult times, reminding them that, with God's guidance and a commitment to working together, healing and renewal are always possible.

Mark and Julia's story reflects that while no marriage is perfect, with God at the center, even the most broken relationships can find hope and new life. Their journey shows that with patience, honesty, and a dedication to faith, a couple can rebuild their bond, discovering a love that's even stronger than before.

Key Lessons Learned and Relatable Experiences

Mark and Julia's journey offers valuable lessons that resonate deeply with couples facing their own challenges. Through their story, we see that healing is rarely a straightforward path—it's filled with moments of struggle, patience, and small victories that ultimately build a stronger, faith-centered relationship. Here are some of the key insights they gained along the way, along with how these experiences might relate to others.

One of the first lessons Mark and Julia learned was that trust must be rebuilt through consistent, transparent actions. Apologies and words of reassurance are a necessary start, but real trust only grows when partners commit to openness and follow through. Mark had to be transparent with his schedule and willingly share details of his day-to-day life to show Julia he was committed to change. Julia, in turn, learned to acknowledge these efforts, even if trust was slow to rebuild. For couples, this is a reminder that trust restoration isn't immediate but is cultivated through small, reliable actions that reinforce a partner's commitment over time.

Open communication became another essential part of their healing. At first, every conversation was heavy with tension and hurt, but they learned the importance of expressing feelings honestly and listening without jumping to conclusions. For many couples, avoiding difficult conversations feels safer, but bottling up thoughts and emotions often leads to misunderstandings. Mark and Julia discovered that creating a safe space where they could share openly without fear of judgment was vital for reconnecting emotionally and understanding each other's needs.

A third key lesson was that forgiveness is often a daily decision. For Julia, forgiving Mark wasn't a single moment of closure; it was a journey that required patience and grace. Some days were harder than others, and on those days, she turned to prayer, asking God for the strength to forgive. Mark, too, learned that forgiveness didn't erase his past actions but allowed them both to focus on building a better future. This lesson highlights that forgiveness is an ongoing process, a daily commitment to let go of resentment and trust in God's plan for healing.

Their faith provided an anchor throughout this journey. Leaning on scripture and prayer gave Mark and Julia strength they couldn't find on their own. They drew comfort from verses like Psalm 34:18, reminding themselves that God was close to them in their pain. For many couples, faith serves as a source of resilience, a way to find peace and purpose even in the darkest moments. Mark and Julia's experience shows that when human strength feels insufficient, turning to God can bring clarity, hope, and the courage to persevere.

A counselor helped Mark and Julia set small, achievable goals instead of overwhelming them with expectations to fix everything at once. This approach gave them confidence, helping them see progress through shared laughter or peaceful conversations. Many couples find that focusing on small steps and celebrating little wins is an effective way to restore their relationship. These moments build momentum and reinforce the idea that positive change is possible, even if it's gradual.

Community and counseling were additional sources of support. Their counselor provided guidance and a safe space for difficult conversations, while their church community offered encouragement through prayer and shared experiences. This external support reminded them that they weren't alone in their journey. Reaching out for help—whether through counseling or a supportive faith community—can be a turning point for couples, providing clarity, hope, and practical guidance.

Ultimately, Mark and Julia learned that love is an active choice, one they had to renew each day. Some days, it came naturally; other days, it took intentional effort. But by choosing to love each other daily, they committed to looking past old wounds and working toward a future based on mutual respect and hope. For couples, this reinforces that love is not merely an emotion but a purposeful choice to prioritize each other, to forgive, and to keep moving forward with patience and kindness.

The lessons in Mark and Julia's story reflect the wisdom that comes from facing challenges head-on with faith and intentionality. Their journey reminds us that healing is possible when both partners are willing to work through their struggles, lean on their faith, and choose each other each day. Through patience, prayer, and a commitment to growth, even the hardest trials can lead to a marriage that's not only restored but stronger than before.

How Faith Played a Role in Each Couple's Journey

Mark and Julia's story illustrates the vital role faith can play in restoring a marriage, showing how reliance on God's love and guidance transforms even the most difficult challenges. Through prayer, scripture, and support from their faith community, they found strength and resilience in moments of doubt, anger, and sorrow. For many couples, faith becomes an anchor, offering a foundation of hope and direction when human efforts fall short.

One of the first ways faith shaped their journey was through Julia's approach to forgiveness. She struggled with hurt and anger but found strength in prayer and scriptures like Ephesians 4:32, which calls believers to forgive as Christ has forgiven. This passage reframed forgiveness for her as an act of grace, not just a decision, giving her the courage to continue healing. Mark, too, leaned on his faith, praying for patience and strength to make amends, knowing that God's grace could help him rebuild what had been broken.

Daily prayer together became another essential practice. Starting each morning in prayer not only gave them a sense of calm but also reminded them that they were united in their faith, even amid hardship. Matthew 18:20, which speaks of God's presence when two or more gather in His name, brought them comfort, helping them feel supported by a higher power. In these quiet moments, they felt their bond strengthening, creating a sense of unity that hadn't been there before.

Trusting in God's plan gave them hope when doubt crept in. Julia often wrestled with questions about whether their marriage could truly be restored, yet Jeremiah 29:11 reminded her that God had plans for them—a future filled with hope. This verse reassured her that their struggle was part of a greater journey, and trusting in God's promises allowed both Julia and Mark to keep moving forward. For Mark, leaning on God's promise of redemption helped him see himself as worthy of forgiveness and change.

Through scripture, they learned to see each other with new eyes. They often read 1 Corinthians 13:4-7, which describes love as patient, kind, and forgiving. This passage inspired them to treat each other with grace, choosing understanding over resentment. Julia learned to appreciate Mark's efforts to rebuild, and Mark acknowledged the strength Julia showed in her journey to forgive. Their faith allowed them to see each other's actions as efforts toward healing, not reminders of past pain.

The support of their faith community also played an Invaluable role. Attending a couples' Bible study connected them with others who had experienced similar struggles, reminding them they weren't alone. Their pastor's prayers and the empathy of friends gave them a sense of belonging and encouragement, especially on tough days. Their community embodied Galatians 6:2, which teaches to "carry each other's burdens," showing Mark and Julia the importance of shared faith and support.

Finally, they committed to regular Bible study as part of their journey. Scriptures like Colossians 3:13, which emphasizes forgiving as the Lord forgives, became reminders of the kind of marriage they wanted to build. Studying God's word gave them both practical guidance and a renewed sense of purpose, realigning their marriage with values rooted in compassion, patience, and love.

Faith transformed Mark and Julia's relationship, guiding them from brokenness to wholeness. Through each step of their journey, they learned that God's love provides the strength to heal, forgive, and grow. Their story is a powerful reminder that, when couples place their trust in God, even the most challenging moments can lead to deeper love, unity, and hope for the future.

Reflection Questions – What Can You Apply from These Stories?

Reflecting on real-life stories like Mark and Julia's offers an opportunity to consider the health of your own relationship and identify practical ways to build a deeper, more resilient connection. Here are some thoughtful reflection questions designed to help you draw meaningful lessons from their experiences, nurturing understanding and growth in your marriage.

1. Are There Areas in Your Marriage Where Trust Needs Rebuilding?
Trust is essential, yet small breaches or unmet expectations can erode it over time. Reflect on any areas where trust might feel strained—whether in communication, finances, or reliability. Identifying these areas can lead to steps toward genuine rebuilding.

Action Step: Openly discuss these trust areas with your spouse, aiming for transparency and honesty. Together, commit to consistent actions that build trust, like keeping communication open and reliable follow-through.

2. How Can You Incorporate Faith into Your Daily Interactions?

Mark and Julia's journey highlighted the role of faith in keeping them centered. Their reliance on prayer, scripture, and God's guidance strengthened their bond. Consider the ways your faith currently impacts your relationship and how you might integrate it more deeply into daily life.

Action Step: Set aside time for a shared prayer or a moment of reflection. Whether it's reading a verse together or praying before meals, these small acts keep your focus on faith and each other.

3. Do You Regularly Communicate in a Way That Fosters Understanding and Growth?

Communication is key, especially in stressful times. Think about your usual communication habits and whether they create mutual understanding or lead to defensiveness. Consider where adjustments might help to create more openness and connection.

Action Step: Practice active listening and try weekly check-ins, where each partner can openly share thoughts and feelings. This practice builds a foundation for honest, constructive dialogue.

4. In What Areas Do You Need to Extend or Receive Forgiveness?

Forgiveness can be challenging but is vital for a strong marriage. Reflect on any past hurts or unresolved issues that might benefit from forgiveness. Releasing resentment can lead to healing and a fresh start.

Action Step: Remember Ephesians 4:32, which calls for compassion and forgiveness. Reflect on whether there are specific hurts you're holding onto, and discuss these with your spouse in the spirit of peace and resolution.

5. How Do You View Your Spouse Through a Lens of Grace and Patience?

It's easy to focus on faults during difficult times, but seeing each other with grace can transform your perspective. Consider how you view your spouse—do you hold on to frustrations, or are you able to see the positives?

Action Step: Aim to recognize and appreciate the good in your spouse. Simple acts of appreciation can shift your relationship, fostering an environment of kindness and understanding.

6. Are You Willing to Seek Help and Support When Needed?
Seeking support through counseling or a church community made a significant difference for Mark and Julia. Reflect on whether you'd be open to external guidance if challenges feel overwhelming. **Action Step:** If you're facing difficulties, reach out to a trusted counselor, pastor, or supportive couple's group. Finding encouragement and wisdom in a safe environment can provide clarity and support.

7. What Steps Can You Take Today to Strengthen Your Marriage?
Consider small actions you could take now to nurture and strengthen your relationship. These don't need to be grand gestures—sometimes, the smallest changes make the biggest impact.

Action Step: Write down a few small actions you can commit to this week, whether it's setting aside time for quality conversation, sharing a prayer, or expressing gratitude. These steps are the building blocks of a resilient marriage.

These reflective questions encourage ongoing dialogue, self-awareness, and commitment, allowing you and your spouse to apply real-life lessons to strengthen your own journey. With each thoughtful step, you can nurture a foundation of trust, love, and faith that supports a thriving marriage through all of life's seasons.

Chapter 7

Guided Reflections and Journaling Prompts

Reflection can be a powerful tool in marriage, offering each partner a chance to understand themselves and each other more deeply. Thoughtful reflection—both individually and together—can uncover valuable insights, promote empathy, and strengthen your connection. This section offers reflection questions designed for both individual and shared reflection, helping each person explore emotions, identify areas for growth, and nurture unity.

Individual Reflection Questions

These questions allow you to explore your personal thoughts, emotions, and experiences in your marriage. Taking time for personal reflection helps build self-awareness and encourages personal growth, both of which positively impact your relationship.

1. What Do I Appreciate Most About My Spouse?

Reflecting on the qualities that first drew you to your partner and those you continue to cherish can rekindle appreciation. When was the last time you shared these feelings openly?

2. Are There Any Past Hurts I'm Holding Onto?

Identify any unresolved disappointments or painful memories that might be creating emotional distance. Letting go of these hurts can open the way to forgiveness and deeper closeness.

3. How Do I Communicate During Conflict?

Think about how you typically respond during disagreements. Do you tend to be honest and open, or do you avoid addressing difficult topics? Recognizing your own communication patterns helps you identify changes for healthier conflict resolution.

4. In What Ways Can I Support My Spouse More?

Reflect on ways you could offer more support, whether through encouraging words, acts of kindness, or shared quality time. These reflections can help you identify ways to nurture your relationship and strengthen your bond.

5. **How Can I Rely More on Faith in My Marriage?**
Consider your spiritual journey and how it influences your relationship. Are there ways you could bring your faith more intentionally into daily interactions and decisions, or into the way you handle challenges together?

Couple Reflection Questions

These questions are intended for shared discussion, fostering open communication and mutual understanding. They create a space to explore each other's perspectives and build a constructive path forward together.

1. **What Are Our Shared Goals as a Couple?**
Discuss your mutual goals, both immediate and long-term, in areas like communication, intimacy, and faith. Reaffirming these goals strengthens your sense of purpose and unity.

2. **How Can We Better Navigate Conflict Together?**
Reflect on your current approach to disagreements. Identify patterns that may need adjustment and brainstorm strategies that work for both of you to handle conflicts more constructively.

3. **What Spiritual Practices Can We Share?**
Explore ways to incorporate your faith into your relationship. This could mean praying together, reading scripture, or attending church as a couple. Sharing spiritual practices reinforces a commitment to mutual spiritual growth.

4. **How Can We Support Each Other's Individual Growth?**
Each partner's journey is unique, and supporting each other's growth brings strength to the relationship. Talk openly about personal goals and how you can support each other's pursuits and dreams.

5. **What Steps Can We Take to Build Lasting Trust?**

Trust is built and strengthened over time. Share ideas on how you can nurture trust in everyday ways through transparency, honesty, and support.

Reflection as a Practice

Making reflection a regular practice—whether individually or together—can strengthen your relationship in meaningful ways. Try setting aside time each week for personal reflection, followed by a shared time where you can come together to discuss your thoughts. This approach nurtures a deeper connection, creating a safe space where both partners feel heard, valued, and supported.

Space for Personal Journaling and Insights

Journaling can be a deeply personal and transformative way to nurture self-awareness, track growth, and deepen intimacy within a marriage. This section encourages both individual and shared journaling practices, helping each spouse process their experiences, clarify emotions, and celebrate progress along the way. As couples reflect on their thoughts and insights, journaling can serve as a powerful reminder of the journey they're on together.

Why Journaling Matters in a Marriage

Journaling creates a private, reflective space for each spouse to explore their feelings openly and honestly. Individually, it provides a way to understand personal emotions, spot patterns, and recognize areas for growth. For couples, it can also be a shared experience—whether through exchanging journal entries or simply discussing what each person has written. This shared practice helps foster a greater sense of trust and understanding.

Marriage is filled with milestones and meaningful moments, both uplifting and challenging. By documenting these experiences, couples can create a lasting record of their journey together. During difficult times, revisiting past entries can serve as a reminder of the resilience they've built, the progress they've made, and the love that has sustained them through various seasons.

Suggested Journaling Prompts for Individual Reflection

These prompts allow each spouse to explore their own thoughts, feelings, and experiences. They're intended to encourage self-awareness and provide a safe outlet for processing personal emotions.

- **What Are My Current Feelings About Our Marriage?**
Take a moment to describe your current emotions about your relationship. Are you feeling supported, content, challenged, or in need of change? This exercise helps you identify where you are emotionally and any unmet needs you may have.

- **What Does Forgiveness Mean to Me?**
Reflect on the role forgiveness plays in your relationship. Are there past hurts you may still be holding onto? Journaling about forgiveness can pave the way toward releasing resentment and finding peace.

- **In What Ways Can I Show Love More Clearly?**
Think about the ways you express love and consider how they align with your spouse's needs. Are there specific actions that would make your love feel more visible? Being intentional about how you express love helps you foster a closer bond.

- **How Do I Handle Conflict, and How Would I Like to Improve?**
Consider your natural approach to disagreements. Do you avoid them, become defensive, or try to resolve them quickly? Reflecting on your tendencies can help you make more intentional choices during future conflicts.

- **What Role Does Faith Play in Our Marriage?**
Reflect on the role of faith in your relationship. Are there areas where you'd like to grow spiritually, either individually or together? Identifying this helps align your relationship with your spiritual values.

Suggested Journaling Prompts for Couple Reflection

These prompts are intended for partners to explore together, encouraging open communication and a shared sense of purpose. Each prompt can be approached individually and then discussed together, fostering understanding and connection.

- **What Are Our Greatest Strengths as a Couple?**

Reflect on the unique qualities that make your relationship strong. Acknowledge the ways you complement each other, and celebrate the strengths that have helped you grow together.

- **How Have We Grown Together Over the Past Year?**

Look back on the past year and identify areas where you've grown. Whether it's in communication, trust, or shared experiences, recognizing your progress reinforces the positive direction of your relationship.

- **What Challenges Do We Face, and How Can We Address Them?**

Identify any ongoing challenges and explore potential solutions together. Writing about these allows both partners to think constructively about the future.

- **What Dreams Do We Share for Our Future?**

Dream together about your future as a couple. Whether it's travel, building a family, or other shared goals, this reflection strengthens your vision and deepens your commitment to each other.

- **How Can We Make Our Faith a Stronger Foundation in Our Marriage?**

Consider how to deepen your spiritual connection. Think about practices like prayer, Bible study, or attending church, and discuss what might bring you closer to God and each other.

Creating a Journaling Routine

To benefit most from journaling, consider setting aside a dedicated time each week to reflect. This could be Sunday evening, a quiet morning, or any time that suits your schedule. Both individual and shared journaling can be meaningful—allowing each spouse to first reflect privately, then come together to discuss insights and reflections.

Sample Journal Entry Setup

- **Date**: Include the date at the top of each entry to track progress over time.
- **Today I Feel...**: Start with a simple statement about your current emotions to anchor the entry.
- **Reflection Prompt Response**: Choose a prompt and write freely without editing. Allow yourself to explore your thoughts openly.
- **Closing Thought or Prayer**: End with a positive thought, intention, or prayer for your marriage to reinforce hope and commitment.

Reflecting on Your Journey Together

Each journal entry captures a unique moment in your marriage, creating a record of your experiences, challenges, and growth. Looking back on these entries over time offers encouragement, reminding you of the steps you've taken together and the foundation of love and faith that continues to strengthen your bond.

Simple Exercises to Apply Lessons Learned in Daily Life

Applying what you've learned through reflection and journaling can bring lasting transformation to your marriage. Practical exercises help turn these insights into actions that strengthen your bond and deepen understanding. These simple, daily practices foster connection, build trust, and bring faith into your everyday relationship.

Daily Gratitude Practice

Each day, take a moment to express something you're grateful for about your spouse—whether it's a kind act, a cherished memory, or a quality you admire. Make this a consistent practice at the start or end of each day. This small, regular expression of gratitude builds a positive focus in your marriage, helping each partner feel appreciated and valued.

Weekly Check-In Conversations

Dedicate 15-20 minutes each week for a "check-in" conversation. During this time, each person shares thoughts, concerns, and ways to offer more support. Use prompts like "What went well this week?" and "Is there anything that needs improvement?" Listening attentively to each other without interruption fosters openness and helps you address concerns before they grow.

Monthly Goal-Setting as a Couple

At the start of each month, sit down together to set a few personal, relational, or spiritual goals—one or two for each person and one shared goal. Place these somewhere visible, like a note on the fridge, to keep your focus on what you're building together. This practice creates a sense of unity and reinforces your shared vision.

Shared Devotional Time

Reserve one evening a week for a shared devotional. Choose a passage, verse, or topic that resonates with both of you. Take turns reading it, discuss its relevance to your relationship, and close with a prayer asking for guidance. This practice deepens spiritual intimacy and reinforces shared values, bringing God into your marriage consistently.

Love Language Practice
Identify each other's love language—Words of Affirmation, Acts of Service, Receiving Gifts, Quality Time, or Physical Touch—and make an intentional effort each day to express love in your spouse's language. At the end of the week, reflect together on how this intentional practice has affected your connection. Meeting each other's emotional needs in this way deepens understanding and shows genuine care.

Conflict Reflection and Prayer
After a disagreement, take time to reflect together on what happened and discuss how you could approach it differently in the future. End with a prayer, asking for patience and wisdom to navigate future challenges. This reflection turns conflict into a learning opportunity and promotes a peaceful resolution.

"Three Wins" Daily Reflection
Each evening, share three positive moments or "wins" from your day—whether a meaningful moment, a small accomplishment, or something thoughtful your spouse did. Reflecting on these positives helps reinforce gratitude and resilience, even during challenging times.

Prayer Journal for Shared Prayers and Goals
Start a shared prayer journal to document your prayers, goals, and any answered prayers. Each week, write a prayer together focused on a specific need or desire for your relationship. Over time, you'll see how prayers have been answered, creating a record of your shared journey in faith.

Integrating these exercises into your routine strengthens the foundation of appreciation, open communication, and faith in your marriage. By taking small, intentional steps each day, you'll find yourselves growing together in understanding and love.

Chapter 8

Special Situations and Life Stages
Handling Conflicts During Major Life Changes

In any marriage, major life changes bring both excitement and challenges. These transitions—whether it's becoming parents, moving to a new city, or starting a new career—can impact how couples communicate and understand each other. During these times, routines shift, roles evolve, and expectations can change, creating stress that often leads to conflict if not thoughtfully addressed. Navigating these shifts together can prevent misunderstandings and, in turn, strengthen the relationship.

The arrival of a child, for instance, is one of the most joyful yet demanding milestones in a marriage. Parenthood brings new responsibilities and adjustments that can affect both partners emotionally and physically. Sleepless nights, diaper changes, and balancing work with childcare become part of everyday life. Couples may find themselves feeling overwhelmed or even resentful if they feel unsupported. To navigate this, regular, open conversations about expectations and each other's needs are essential. Scheduling weekly check-ins provides a safe time to express appreciation, discuss challenges, and explore ways to support each other. Discussing and dividing childcare and household tasks based on each partner's current energy and strengths is helpful, especially as each partner's needs fluctuate over time. Above all, it's important to remember the value of the partnership itself, which can sometimes be overshadowed by the demands of parenthood. A simple date night or even a few uninterrupted moments at the end of the day to reconnect helps preserve the bond between partners.

Job changes—whether a promotion, a new position, or even an unexpected job loss—can bring both excitement and stress. New roles may bring longer hours, different responsibilities, and financial changes that impact a couple's shared daily life. Without clear communication, the adjustments can create tension. Open conversations about expectations go a long way; discussing how new responsibilities might impact routines, time spent together, or even household roles can help set realistic expectations. Supporting each other's growth is also key; it might mean celebrating small career victories or offering extra help at home during high-stress periods. Additionally, setting healthy boundaries for work can be especially important—agreeing to "no-work zones" or times to unplug can ensure that work doesn't overshadow the relationship.

Relocation, too, brings both challenges and opportunities. Moving to a new city, state, or country can mean adapting to a different environment, establishing routines, and forming new social connections. The stress of adjusting to a new home, job, or community can sometimes put strain on the relationship, especially if one partner feels more comfortable with the change than the other. Talking openly about feelings and any fears—without judgment—allows each partner to feel supported, whether they're feeling excited or a bit homesick. Establishing shared routines can also help create a sense of stability; exploring the neighborhood together, finding new favorite spots, or creating a comforting setup at home can make the adjustment easier. Building a support network, like connecting with a local church or social group, provides additional emotional support and a sense of community in the new environment.

Many life transitions bring financial adjustments—whether due to a change in income, increased expenses, or new responsibilities. Finances are a sensitive topic for many couples, and when life shifts, financial concerns can quickly lead to stress and misunderstandings if not discussed openly. Regular, honest discussions about finances create a shared understanding, helping to prevent tension down the road. Agreeing on shared goals and setting a budget that aligns with the new reality can also foster a sense of partnership and clarity. For example, managing a change in income or addressing unexpected expenses can feel less overwhelming when both partners feel involved and informed. Turning to faith during these times, by praying together for wisdom and provision, can also provide peace and remind both partners that their ultimate provider is God.

Every life stage brings unique challenges, but by keeping communication open, supporting each other's needs, and seeking God's guidance, couples can weather these transitions together. Facing conflicts during major transitions proactively can turn challenges into moments of growth, drawing partners closer in unity and understanding.

Navigating Differences in Cultural and Family Backgrounds

In marriage, each partner brings a unique set of cultural, family, and personal experiences that shape their values, traditions, and expectations. These differences can enrich a relationship by adding diverse perspectives and traditions to celebrate, but they can also lead to misunderstandings if left unaddressed. Recognizing and respecting each other's backgrounds can help couples turn these differences into strengths, deepening their bond rather than creating tension.

When two people from different cultural backgrounds come together, they bring along values, traditions, and perspectives that may not always align. Even within the same culture, family traditions and personal beliefs can differ significantly. From how holidays are celebrated to dietary preferences and financial values, understanding each other's cultural context can help reduce potential conflicts. Open dialogue is essential here. Taking time to share stories, family traditions, and personal experiences allows both partners to appreciate where the other is coming from. Celebrating these differences together can also help, whether by creating shared traditions or finding ways to honor each other's culture. When each partner feels respected in what matters to them, it builds a strong foundation of mutual appreciation.

Family dynamics also play a large role in shaping how we approach relationships. Each partner may come from a family with its own style of communication, conflict resolution, and boundaries. These differences can sometimes create friction, especially if in-laws have specific expectations or if family traditions come into play. Setting boundaries together as a couple can help manage these dynamics. By discussing family expectations openly, couples can agree on what boundaries they need to maintain a balanced relationship. It's also helpful to approach family attachments with understanding, rather than criticism. Supporting each other in family matters and creating a unified front when needed strengthens the couple's bond and communicates to both families that the marriage is a priority.

Communication styles can vary widely between cultures and families. Some families may encourage open, direct communication, while others prioritize politeness and restraint. Misunderstandings are common if partners assume their own way of communicating is the "right" way. Identifying communication preferences and actively listening to each other's perspectives helps couples bridge these differences. Listening without interrupting and reflecting back what was heard shows respect for each other's style, helping to build trust. Working together to find a communication approach that balances both preferences is key to maintaining harmony. For example, if one partner prefers directness and the other values a gentler approach, agreeing on a respectful middle ground can prevent conflict and strengthen understanding.

Differences in cultural or family backgrounds can sometimes lead to conflict, especially if they involve unaddressed assumptions about roles or traditions. Whether it's differing views on parenting, finances, or family roles, these conflicts can be managed by recognizing that each person's background holds value. Approaching these conflicts with a mindset of learning, rather than judgment, can turn disagreements into opportunities for growth. Looking for areas of common ground, where backgrounds overlap, can also be helpful, as it creates a foundation for compromise and mutual respect. During moments of tension, bringing these issues before God in prayer can also bring comfort and guidance. Praying for unity and understanding allows couples to approach challenges with patience, remembering that their union is purposeful and blessed.

Every marriage is an opportunity to create a new family culture together. A healthy relationship balances the traditions and values of both partners, blending them to create something unique. Talking about the values you want to prioritize together and choosing traditions that feel meaningful can make each partner feel included. Establishing new traditions that reflect both backgrounds helps build a shared identity and can be as simple as celebrating different holidays or creating family rituals that celebrate both cultures.

Embracing cultural and family differences in marriage adds depth and richness to the relationship. With respect, patience, and open communication, couples can navigate these differences gracefully, building a marriage that honors both backgrounds and paves the way for a unified future.

Balancing Work Commitments with Marriage Responsibilities

Balancing the demands of a career with the responsibilities of marriage can be challenging for many couples. As work schedules become more demanding, personal connections often take a back seat, leading to feelings of neglect and disconnection. Successfully navigating these challenges requires clear communication, mutual support, and a commitment to prioritizing the relationship alongside professional obligations.

One of the biggest challenges is letting work spill into home life. Checking emails after hours, bringing work stress home, or allowing work schedules to interfere with family time can strain the relationship. Setting boundaries between work and home helps create a clear distinction, ensuring that time together is focused and meaningful. Couples can establish "no-work zones" in their home, such as agreeing not to discuss or engage in work activities during meals or in the bedroom, creating spaces that are solely for each other. Agreeing on a cutoff time for work-related activities each evening can also protect personal time, allowing both partners to unwind and reconnect. Mutual respect for each other's time means understanding when work is a priority but also knowing when to put it aside to nurture the relationship.

Planning quality time in advance can help ensure the relationship remains a priority. With busy work schedules, spontaneous moments together can be rare, so scheduling time together intentionally can make a significant difference. Weekly or monthly dates can be as simple as a coffee date, a walk in the park, or a cozy evening at home. Small, daily check-ins, even a quick "how was your day?" over a cup of tea, keep communication lines open and show your partner that you're thinking of them. Planning vacations or mini-breaks, even if just for a weekend, provides both of you with an opportunity to escape daily responsibilities and reconnect. These regular moments help reinforce your commitment to each other, even in the midst of demanding work schedules.

Supporting each other's career goals is essential for maintaining a balanced relationship. When one partner is facing a busy period at work, the other may need to step up in certain areas at home, fostering teamwork and understanding. Communicating openly about career aspirations helps each partner understand what the other is working toward, creating a sense of shared purpose. Flexibility during busy seasons—whether it's covering extra responsibilities at home or offering emotional support—demonstrates a commitment to each other's growth. Celebrating each other's achievements, both big and small, also strengthens the bond, making each person feel valued and appreciated.

Managing work-related stress is another key aspect of balancing work and marriage. Stress from work can easily spill over into home life if not managed properly. To prevent this, create a "decompression time" after work—whether it's taking a few minutes to relax, going for a short walk, or doing something calming. Allowing each other time to unwind before diving into household or relationship responsibilities helps both partners approach the evening with a clear mind. Limiting work-related discussions to a set time, such as 10–15 minutes, can also keep work from overshadowing personal moments. Practicing stress-relief activities together, like exercising or enjoying a peaceful evening routine, fosters a shared sense of relaxation and connection.

Faith can play a pivotal role in helping couples balance work and marriage. Praying together for wisdom and guidance helps couples focus on what truly matters and seek God's help in managing their commitments. Praying for wisdom on how to allocate time and energy can provide a sense of peace, especially during busy periods. Trusting that God is ultimately in control of both your work and your marriage can ease anxiety, reminding you that He will provide for all your needs. Attending faith-based workshops focused on balancing career and family life from a Christian perspective can also offer insights and strengthen your commitment to a balanced, God-centered marriage.

Balancing work and marriage requires ongoing communication, flexibility, and support. By setting clear boundaries, scheduling quality time, supporting each other's career goals, and integrating faith into your routines, you can manage work responsibilities without sacrificing the relationship. Prioritizing each other amid professional demands reinforces the bond, creating a marriage that thrives even during the busiest times.

Practical Advice Tailored to Each Stage

Each stage of marriage is marked by its own unique blend of joys, challenges, and opportunities for growth. Whether newlyweds, raising young children, navigating midlife transitions, or enjoying the golden years, each phase calls for adjustments in how couples communicate, support one another, and nurture their connection. Here are practical insights tailored to each stage of marriage to help couples strengthen their bond with mutual respect, understanding, and a shared purpose.

In the early days of marriage, excitement and discovery often set the tone for laying a strong foundation. This is a valuable time to establish healthy habits in communication and mutual support, creating a base for years to come. Newlyweds benefit from prioritizing open communication—making it a habit to discuss both big and small issues openly, from finances to long-term goals. Setting boundaries with extended family can help too, ensuring that each person feels supported as they build a life together. And by creating routines, whether through weekly date nights or evening check-ins, couples can maintain a rhythm that keeps them closely connected.

When young children come into the picture, marriage takes on a new dimension of responsibility and joy. Parenting demands can easily overshadow the relationship if couples aren't intentional about carving out time for each other. Parents of young children can prioritize couple time, even if it's just a short chat in the evening or a weekend outing, which helps maintain intimacy. Sharing the load as a team by dividing household and parenting tasks and communicating openly about needs can reduce misunderstandings, building a stable family environment rooted in mutual support.

Midlife brings shifts as children become more independent, and many couples find themselves juggling career growth, health considerations, and future planning. This stage offers a chance to encourage both personal and mutual growth by supporting each other's interests and even exploring new hobbies together. Reassessing financial goals and health priorities is also essential in this phase, ensuring both partners feel aligned as they look toward the future. Staying physically and emotionally well also strengthens each partner's ability to adapt and be present for one another as roles evolve.

For empty nesters, this season can be about rediscovering each other. With more time and fewer parenting responsibilities, couples have the freedom to focus on romance and shared goals once again. Rekindling intimacy and setting new dreams, whether through travel, learning a skill, or volunteering, helps bring fresh excitement to the relationship. Celebrating the journey you've traveled together and looking back on achievements strengthens the connection, adding richness to this new phase of companionship.

The golden years are a time to reflect on a life well-shared and enjoy the fruits of hard work. With a quieter schedule, couples can embrace simple pleasures, from morning coffee together to leisurely walks. Staying socially active by maintaining relationships with family, community, and friends provides a sense of purpose and engagement. Many couples use this time to focus on creating a legacy, whether through mentoring, family traditions, or shared stories of faith that inspire future generations.

As couples age, health and well-being can become more prominent aspects of daily life. Supporting each other through any health challenges, adapting to changing needs, and celebrating life's simple joys together fosters resilience and a deeper companionship. Encouraging a lifestyle that supports each partner's health and well-being and adapting to new responsibilities as needed keeps the marriage steady. This season invites partners to cherish each moment, finding gratitude in the companionship they share.

Embracing each stage of marriage with openness, empathy, and faith builds a relationship that thrives through every season. These practical insights serve as a roadmap, guiding couples through the unique experiences that each phase brings, strengthening their bond and commitment as they journey through life together.

Chapter 9

Prayers and Scriptures for Conflict and Growth

Prayers for Common Situations, Such as Overcoming Anger or Seeking Peace

Prayer is a powerful way to invite God's guidance into the heart of a marriage, helping couples navigate challenges with grace and love. Whether in moments of frustration, times of need, or joyful celebration, turning to God allows couples to find strength, clarity, and peace. Here are specific prayers for common situations that can help anchor a relationship in faith, allowing God's presence to fill each moment.

When anger takes hold, it's easy to say things that hurt. Anger clouds our judgment and often prevents us from seeing the situation clearly. This prayer for overcoming anger is a way to pause and ask God for calm and clarity, creating space for compassion to replace frustration.

"Dear Lord, I'm feeling overwhelmed by anger, and I know this isn't what You want for my heart. Help me to release these feelings and replace them with peace and patience. Guide my words and actions so that I may respond to my spouse with kindness, even when I feel hurt or frustrated. Soften my heart, Lord, and help me see beyond my anger, so I can understand and show compassion. Grant me the strength to forgive and approach conflict with a spirit of love. In Jesus' name, Amen."

In moments of conflict or uncertainty, our hearts can feel unsettled. Seeking peace allows us to approach our relationship with patience and grace. This prayer invites God's calming presence to fill our hearts and homes.

"Heavenly Father, my heart feels troubled, and I'm weighed down by the challenges we're facing. I ask for Your peace to fill my heart, giving me the strength to approach our relationship with patience and grace. Help me to release my worries, trusting that You are guiding us. Lord, grant us both peace in our hearts and minds, so we may approach each other

with calm and understanding. Let Your presence be our anchor as we navigate this season. In Your name, Amen."

Patience is a foundational element in marriage, allowing us to listen closely, respond with love, and show grace even in difficult times. This prayer asks for God's help in cultivating patience and understanding so that we can better serve each other.

"Dear God, I come to You seeking patience and understanding. Help me to listen to my spouse with an open heart and respond with kindness, even when I feel frustrated. Give me the strength to set aside my pride and focus on building a deeper connection. Teach me to be slow to anger, quick to forgive, and always ready to show love. May Your patience fill my heart, guiding my thoughts and actions. Thank You, Lord, for the gift of my spouse and the lessons we're learning together. In Jesus' name, Amen."

Forgiveness is central to healing in marriage, allowing partners to release past hurts and move forward. This prayer focuses on letting go of resentment and seeking reconciliation, with God's grace as the foundation.

"Lord, I'm struggling with feelings of hurt and resentment. Help me let go of these feelings and choose forgiveness. Remind me that You have forgiven me time and time again and that I am called to extend that same grace to my spouse. Heal the wounds between us, Lord, and guide us toward reconciliation. May we find strength in Your love and work together to restore harmony in our relationship. In Your precious name, Amen."

During difficult times, when life's challenges feel heavy, we rely on God's strength to persevere. This prayer invites God to be our source of resilience, helping us stand together and trust in His guidance.

"Dear Heavenly Father, we are facing difficult times, and we feel the weight of our struggles. I ask for Your strength to sustain us, to give us courage, and to remind us that we're not alone. Help us rely on each other and find hope in Your promises. May we face each challenge with

faith, knowing that You are by our side, guiding us through every obstacle. Strengthen our love, Lord, and let Your presence be our source of comfort and resilience. In Jesus' name, Amen."

These prayers offer a way to turn to God in both times of need and times of gratitude. Praying together or individually invites God's peace and strength into the marriage, creating a foundation of faith that supports each couple's journey. Through prayer, couples find reassurance that God walks with them through every season, shaping their relationship with love and grace.

Go-to Bible Passages for Strength and Guidance

The Bible is filled with wisdom that speaks directly to the heart of marriage, offering insights and comfort for the unique challenges that couples face. In moments of difficulty, stress, or even celebration, turning to scripture can remind us of God's promises and guide us in building a relationship grounded in love, patience, and unity. Here are key passages that offer strength, encouragement, and perspective for couples navigating the ups and downs of married life.

Philippians 4:6-7 encourages us to find peace even amid life's uncertainties. **"Do not be anxious about anything, but in every situation, by prayer and petition, with thanksgiving, present your requests to God. And the peace of God, which transcends all understanding, will guard your hearts and your minds in Christ Jesus."** Anxiety can creep in, especially when challenges feel overwhelming. This verse reminds us to surrender our worries to God, trusting that His peace will replace our fears. By coming together in prayer, couples can find calm and clarity, allowing God to guide their relationship.

Ephesians 4:2-3 speaks to the heart of humility and patience: **"Be completely humble and gentle; be patient, bearing with one another in love. Make every effort to keep the unity of the Spirit through the bond of peace."** This verse encourages spouses to approach one another with gentleness, even when frustrations arise. By making an effort to show grace and patience, couples can create an atmosphere of respect and understanding, setting a foundation for resolving conflict with love.

James 1:19 offers wisdom on listening: **"Everyone should be quick to listen, slow to speak and slow to become angry."** Listening is a powerful tool for connection. This verse reminds us to give space to our partner's thoughts and feelings before reacting. Practicing active listening fosters respect and deepens trust, helping couples communicate with empathy and avoid unnecessary misunderstandings.

Colossians 3:13 teaches the importance of forgiveness: **"Bear with each other and forgive one another if any of you has a grievance against someone. Forgive as the Lord forgave you."** Holding onto resentment can create distance in a relationship, but God calls us to forgive freely. Choosing forgiveness allows couples to move forward together, restoring unity and trust. Embracing forgiveness, even when it's difficult, is a powerful step toward healing and peace.

1 Corinthians 13:4-7 defines love as patience and kindness: **"Love is patient, love is kind... It always protects, always trusts, always hopes, always perseveres."** This passage captures the essence of true love, which is selfless, enduring, and resilient. In marriage, these qualities—patience, kindness, and humility—help couples build a bond that can withstand life's challenges. Returning to this passage as a guide can inspire spouses to approach each other with renewed love and commitment.

Proverbs 15:1 speaks to the power of gentle words: **"A gentle answer turns away wrath, but a harsh word stirs up anger."** In moments of tension, responding with kindness rather than sharpness can change the tone of a conversation. Gentle communication fosters mutual respect, helping each partner feel valued and understood. Choosing words with care is a simple but impactful way to keep love at the center of interactions.

Matthew 19:6 reminds us of the unity of marriage: "So they are no longer two, but one flesh. Therefore what God has joined together, let no one separate." This verse emphasizes the sacred nature of marriage, emphasizing that it's a bond created by God. Seeing marriage as a spiritual partnership helps couples face challenges as a united team, committed to protecting and nurturing their union.

These passages offer guidance and encouragement that can strengthen a marriage, bringing God's peace and wisdom into daily life. By turning to scripture, couples can find practical ways to address conflicts, foster understanding, and reinforce their bond. God's word serves as a steady reminder of His love and support, inspiring couples to grow together in faith, patience, and mutual respect.

Encouragement to Maintain Regular Prayer and Scripture Reading

Regular prayer, scripture reading, and shared worship form the spiritual backbone of a strong, enduring marriage. These practices provide daily opportunities to invite God's presence into the relationship, fostering growth, unity, and resilience. By committing to these habits, couples nurture their own faith and build a relationship that is spiritually grounded and guided by God's love.

1. The Power of Regular Prayer Together
Prayer brings a sense of peace, vulnerability, and connection. When couples pray together, they open their hearts to God and to each other, creating a bond that strengthens their relationship. Prayer invites God's wisdom, protection, and guidance, and it fosters an environment where both partners feel valued and supported.

Practical Ideas for Consistent Prayer:

- **Set a Regular Time for Prayer:** Establish a specific time each day to pray together. Whether in the morning, before bed, or over a meal, consistency helps make prayer a natural part of your routine.
- **Create a Prayer List:** Write down specific intentions and revisit them together regularly. Celebrate answered prayers and continue to

pray for ongoing needs, building faith and gratitude as you see God's work in your lives.

- **Include Short Prayers Throughout the Day:** In addition to dedicated prayer time, say brief prayers as opportunities arise. Whether it's a moment of gratitude or a quick request for peace, these small prayers weave faith throughout your day.

2. Reading Scripture as a Couple

The Bible offers wisdom that strengthens marriage, guiding couples through every season of life. Reading scripture together brings shared insights, opportunities for growth, and encouragement. This practice allows both partners to explore God's word and reflect on how it applies to their daily lives and relationship.

Practical Ideas for Scripture Reading Together:

- **Choose a Devotional or Reading Plan:** A structured devotional or Bible reading plan offers consistency and focus, especially if it centers on marriage or personal growth.
- **Discuss Each Passage:** After reading, take a few minutes to share thoughts. Discuss how the passage resonates with each of you or how it can be applied in daily life. These discussions deepen understanding and foster connection.
- **Keep a Scripture Journal:** Record meaningful verses, reflections, or insights in a shared journal. This collection becomes a treasured reminder of your growth, something you can revisit for encouragement and inspiration.

3. Strengthening Faith Through Shared Worship

Attending church and worshiping together enhances spiritual unity. Worshiping as a couple brings joy, a sense of community, and accountability, and it reinforces the couple's commitment to their faith and each other.

Practical Ideas for Shared Worship:

- **Attend Church Together Regularly:** Make attending services a shared commitment. Time spent in God's house reinforces your relationship with Him and offers space to grow in faith together.
- **Join a Small Group or Bible Study:** Participate in a small group for married couples or families. These groups provide encouragement, support, and learning from others who share similar values and experiences.
- **Create Worship Activities at Home:** Worship together at home through hymns, Psalms, or Christian music. These simple practices turn your home into a place of faith and peace, inviting God's presence into your shared space.

4. Building a Legacy of Faith in Your Marriage

By nurturing regular prayer, scripture reading, and worship, couples create a legacy of faith that extends beyond their relationship. The faith and love they display become a testimony for future generations, demonstrating the stability and joy that come from a Christ-centered marriage.

Practical Ideas for Building a Faith Legacy:

- **Model Consistency in Prayer and Bible Reading:** Let your commitment to these practices be an example to family, especially children, so they see the strength that comes from a faith-centered life.
- **Share Testimonies of God's Work:** Speak openly about how God has shaped your relationship. Sharing your story encourages others and shows how faith can transform a marriage.
- **Create Faith Traditions:** Establish traditions that focus on faith, such as family prayer nights, reading scripture during special occasions, or incorporating faith into holiday celebrations.

Together, regular prayer, scripture reading, and worship create a lasting spiritual bond that strengthens marriage. These habits invite God's love, wisdom, and presence into every aspect of life, empowering couples to face challenges with grace and build a relationship rooted in His promises. Embracing these practices allows couples to grow in faith, unity, and resilience, creating a legacy of love that endures.

Chapter 10

Sustaining Growth and Strength in Marriage

Tips for Continuous Improvement and Building a Strong Foundation

A strong, enduring marriage thrives on intentional care and continuous growth. Just as a plant requires consistent nurturing, a marriage flourishes when both partners invest in its well-being every day. The following tips provide practical ways to keep building and reinforcing the foundation of your relationship, ensuring it remains resilient, loving, and anchored in faith.

Prioritize Time Together

In the midst of life's demands, quality time can easily slip away, yet it's vital for staying connected. Dedicating intentional time to each other—without distractions—helps nurture understanding, respect, and intimacy. This could be as simple as sharing a meal, taking a walk, or enjoying an evening without devices. The goal is to make each other feel seen and valued.

Practical Steps:

- **Schedule Regular Date Nights:** Treat date nights as essential and put them on the calendar. Prioritizing these moments strengthens your bond and lets you both unwind and connect in a relaxed setting.
- **Plan Weekend Check-Ins:** Take a few minutes each weekend to talk about the week's highs and lows. This routine helps you stay aligned and address small concerns before they grow into larger issues.

Practice Gratitude Daily

Gratitude shifts your focus toward the positive aspects of your marriage. By regularly appreciating each other, you reinforce your bond and keep each other's strengths in view. Expressing gratitude is a reminder of the love and support you both bring to the relationship.

Practical Steps:

- **Share Daily Gratitudes:** Make it a habit to tell your spouse one thing you appreciate about them each day. It could be something simple, like their kindness or a small gesture they made.
- **Keep a Gratitude Journal Together:** Record moments of gratitude in a shared journal. Looking back on these entries reinforces positive feelings and serves as a reminder of God's blessings in your life together.

Embrace Conflict as an Opportunity for Growth

Disagreements are a natural part of any marriage. It's not about avoiding conflict but learning how to address it constructively. By approaching disagreements as moments to learn and grow, you can deepen your understanding of each other and foster a more resilient relationship.

Practical Steps:

- **Practice Active Listening:** During disagreements, listen closely to your spouse's perspective. Reflecting back what you've heard not only ensures clarity but also shows respect for their feelings and point of view.
- **Pause Before Responding:** When emotions are high, take a moment to pause, pray, or gather your thoughts. This practice helps prevent hasty reactions and creates a space for more thoughtful, constructive conversation.

Regularly Reaffirm Your Commitment

Commitment is the cornerstone of a strong marriage. By regularly expressing your love and dedication to each other, you reinforce a sense of stability and trust. Simple gestures and words that affirm your bond can remind both of you of the promises you've made and the journey you're on together.

Practical Steps:

- **Speak Words of Affirmation Often:** Use kind words, written notes, or small gestures to show your love and commitment. These affirmations strengthen your connection and provide reassurance.
- **Celebrate Anniversaries and Milestones:** Marking special moments allows you to reflect on your journey, appreciate the memories you've created, and set goals for the future.

Seek Spiritual Growth Together

A Christ-centered marriage invites God's presence into your relationship, providing wisdom, peace, and strength. Pursuing spiritual growth as a couple draws you closer, aligns your lives with God's will, and helps you navigate life's challenges with faith and grace.

Practical Steps:

- **Pray Together Daily:** Start or end your day with a shared prayer, asking for God's guidance and protection over your marriage.
- **Read the Bible Together:** Make time for scripture reading as a couple. Discussing passages and their relevance to your relationship reinforces shared values and provides guidance from God's word.

By intentionally investing in quality time, gratitude, constructive communication, commitment, and shared faith, you're creating a marriage that is resilient, joyful, and deeply rooted. These practices help you build a solid foundation that will sustain and strengthen your bond for years to come, ensuring your relationship thrives with each new day.

Emphasizing the Importance of Mentorship and Community Support

Marriage is a journey that's best traveled with support, encouragement, and guidance from others. Embracing mentorship and building a community of couples can be transformative, offering strength during challenges and joy during celebrations. A mentor couple—someone who has weathered the seasons of married life—brings invaluable perspective and encouragement, while a community of couples provides a network for mutual learning and growth. Together, mentorship and community reinforce that a thriving marriage is part of a larger story, one of shared faith, purpose, and unity.

The Value of Mentorship in Marriage

A mentor couple serves as a guiding light, offering insights gained through years of experience. They provide a safe space to share struggles, learn from practical wisdom, and gain spiritual guidance rooted in real-life situations. Knowing there's someone who has faced similar trials and triumphed offers comfort and equips you with tools to navigate your own journey.

Benefits of Mentorship:

- **Experienced Guidance:** Mentor couples can share what worked for them, along with what didn't. Their insights come from personal experience, helping you avoid pitfalls and build a lasting foundation.
- **Encouragement and Accountability:** Having a mentor who prays for you and cheers you on reinforces your commitment to growth. Regular check-ins bring a sense of support and keep you focused on the values that guide your marriage.
- **A Safe Space for Vulnerability:** With a mentor couple, you can be honest and open without fear of judgment. This transparency fosters healing and deeper understanding within your marriage.

Practical Steps for Finding a Mentor Couple:

- **Connect Through Your Church:** Many churches offer mentorship programs. Talk to your pastor or church leaders who can help connect you with a seasoned couple.
- **Look Within Your Community:** If formal programs aren't available, reach out to respected couples you know. Older couples are often honored to be asked and more than willing to share their wisdom.
- **Set Regular Meeting Times:** Plan to meet monthly or bi-monthly with your mentor couple to discuss challenges and questions. Establishing a schedule helps make mentorship a reliable part of your marriage journey.

Building a Supportive Community of Couples

A community of couples brings a sense of belonging and shared accountability. Being part of a group allows you to share experiences, exchange advice, and find encouragement during both joyful and challenging times. These friendships remind you that marriage is a shared journey, and they create a supportive network that strengthens your bond.

Benefits of Community Support:

- **Shared Wisdom and Encouragement:** Learning from other couples broadens your perspective, offering fresh insights into common challenges.
- **Celebrating Milestones Together:** Marking anniversaries, family events, and shared moments with other couples reinforces the joy of married life and strengthens bonds.
- **Collective Faith Growth:** Couples' groups often participate in Bible studies, worship, and prayer sessions, creating a space for shared spiritual growth that strengthens both individual relationships and the group as a whole.

Practical Steps for Building a Supportive Couples Community:

- **Join a Small Group or Bible Study:** Many churches offer groups specifically for married couples, focusing on topics relevant to marriage. These groups provide a structured way to build connections.
- **Host Informal Gatherings:** Organize dinners or game nights with other couples. These relaxed settings encourage meaningful conversations and lasting friendships.
- **Attend Marriage Retreats or Workshops:** Participating in marriage retreats or workshops allows you to meet other couples committed to nurturing their marriages, creating bonds that continue beyond the event.

Reaching Out During Difficult Times

Every marriage goes through seasons that feel overwhelming. During these times, mentorship and community support can be a lifeline, offering comfort, guidance, and hope. Reaching out for help reflects a commitment to growth. Trusted friends and mentors provide practical support and prayer, helping you stay grounded and united through tough times.

Practical Steps for Seeking Help in Tough Seasons:

- **Reach Out to Your Mentor Couple:** If a challenging situation arises, turn to your mentors. They can offer immediate support, practical guidance, and prayer.
- **Confide in Trusted Friends:** If you've built a community of trusted couples, consider sharing your struggles with a few close friends. Their support can make all the difference.
- **Engage in Church Support Services:** Many churches offer counseling, prayer teams, and other support services for couples. Don't hesitate to reach out to these resources if you need additional help.

Mentorship and community provide a foundation of support, guidance, and resilience in marriage. Surrounding yourselves with people who share your values builds a network that encourages growth and joy, and reminds you that marriage is part of a larger journey of faith. These connections enrich your relationship, helping you build a marriage that is strong, enduring, and blessed.

Final Reflections on Keeping God at the Center of Your Marriage

A marriage built on God's love and guidance becomes a partnership that can withstand any season or challenge. Keeping God at the center of a marriage invites His wisdom, grace, and purpose into daily life, creating a foundation that is strong and resilient. A marriage grounded in faith becomes a journey of love, patience, forgiveness, and selflessness—qualities that reflect God's own nature. As couples prioritize God in their relationship, they allow His presence to influence every decision, every interaction, and every moment.

Recognizing God as the foundation of your marriage transforms how you approach both the joyful and challenging aspects of life together. A relationship that honors God's purpose remains steadfast, even in difficult times, because it rests on the understanding that marriage is part of a divine plan. By remembering that God is the architect of your marriage, you're reminded that your commitment is sacred, guided by a calling higher than yourselves.

One of the most effective ways to keep God at the center of your relationship is through daily prayer and scripture reading. These practices connect you to God's wisdom, providing a constant source of comfort and direction. Couples who make prayer and scripture a shared experience cultivate a deep spiritual bond that enriches their love and helps them face any challenges with a sense of peace and unity.

Starting and ending each day with prayer as a couple reinforces this connection to God. Whether it's a simple prayer of gratitude, a request for guidance, or a petition for peace, praying together keeps you aligned with God's purpose and reminds you to seek His strength. Reading scripture together also brings new insights and perspectives, helping both partners grow in their faith and deepen their understanding of each other.

In marriage, it's natural to want control, especially when facing uncertainty. But true peace comes from surrendering control to God and trusting in His plan. When couples let go of the need to manage every outcome, they find a calm assurance, knowing that God's wisdom is far greater than their own. Surrendering to God together strengthens a marriage by teaching both partners to rely on His guidance and to support each other through faith.

In moments of doubt, remind each other of God's faithfulness. Reflect on times when He has provided, protected, and led you, and let these memories strengthen your faith. By surrendering your plans to Him, you're not just relinquishing control—you're actively inviting His love and wisdom into your life. This practice builds resilience, knowing that no matter what lies ahead, you're in God's hands.

A marriage centered on God naturally reflects His love, not only between husband and wife but also to those around them. Small acts of kindness, a forgiving spirit, and a commitment to serving others make a marriage a living example of God's love. Through patience and compassion, couples show that their bond is anchored in something greater than themselves, inspiring others and honoring God's presence in their lives.

Celebrate the ways God has blessed your marriage by marking special milestones together. Take time on anniversaries or meaningful dates to reflect on how far you've come and to thank God for guiding your journey. Sharing your story with others, especially couples who may be struggling, can be a powerful testament to God's ability to heal, strengthen, and bless relationships. By opening up about how God has shaped your marriage, you inspire others to seek Him in their own lives.

Ultimately, a marriage centered on God is a relationship that is rich, resilient, and fulfilling. By prioritizing faith, prayer, and a commitment to God's will, couples create a bond that is both deeply spiritual and profoundly joyful. This dedication to keeping God at the heart of the relationship turns marriage into a true partnership, one that reflects His love and stands as a lasting testament to His grace and purpose.